LIFE EXPECTANCIES

LIFE EXPECTANCIES

Monologues That Challenge

Michael Kearns

HEINEMANN
Portsmouth, NH

Heinemann
A division of Reed Elsevier Inc.
361 Hanover Street
Portsmouth, NH 03801–3912
www.heinemanndrama.com

Offices and agents throughout the world

Performance rights information can be found on p. 98.

Cataloging-in-Publication data is on file at the Library of Congress.
ISBN 0-325-00831-0

Editor: Lisa A. Barnett
Production: Vicki Kasabian
Cover design: Jenny Jensen Greenleaf
Typesetter: Tom Allen, Pear Graphic Design
Manufacturing: Steve Bernier

Printed in the United States of America on acid-free paper
09 08 07 06 05 VP 1 2 3 4 5

Contents

BARRIERS (2003)

MAKE LOVE NOT WAR (2005)

Acknowledgments

There are many people who are on my team, individuals who believe in me with a higher degree of passion than I sometimes give myself. These supporting players have influenced the course of my life expectancy with their unflagging respect and unconditional encouragement. Without them, there would be no "second act" and no second collection of monologues. They include James Cronin, Dale Raoul, Raymond Thompson, Carol Preston, Mollie Lowery, Carol Welty, Art Stephens, Bill Spradlin, Zo Harris, Bill Chrisley, David Roman, Karen Skinner, Joan Lipkin, Jenny Sullivan, Tim Miller, and (last, but by no means, least) my brilliant editor, Lisa Barnett.

Introduction

So many astonishing and powerful events have transpired during my life, many of them totally unexpected. Fictitiously woven throughout the monologues contained in *Life Expectancies* are a number of the surprises and jolts and shocks that I've personally weathered and miraculously survived. Perhaps it is those unexpected shifts and changes that shape who we become. Whether responding to unpredictable triumphs or random tragedies, it is that which we don't anticipate, or don't think that we can cope with, that ultimately make us tick.

Even when one chooses an unconventional path, there are expectations that define how we respond to the twists and turns that mark the journey. As a gay man, I never could have imagined finding myself in the midst of a plague that would rob me of most of my buddies and play havoc with my own life expectancy.

When I completed *T-Cells & Sympathy*, a collection of monologues infused with AIDS consciousness, my life expectancy was likely a couple of years tops. That was almost ten years ago.

Among the scenarios that changed the course of my life since that time were the triumphant adoption of my daughter, the mixed blessing of protease inhibitors, the precarious emotional, spiritual, and political state of the gay male community, and finally, the searing immorality of the war in Iraq.

Culled from six theatrepieces I've written over the past decade (*Attachments, Who's Afraid of Edward Albee?, Tell-Tale Kisses, Complications, Barriers,* and *Make Love Not War*), *Life Expectancies* shares many of the themes that drive the first collection of monologues: the battle to overcome discrimination and marginalization, a divisiveness that is destroying America.

Most of my characters have, through monumental personal drama, earned a sense of self-acceptance; not by being perfect but rather by being themselves, in spite of their deep wounds. I invite the actors who take these characters on and the audiences who witness them to avoid judgment and afford them the respect they have allowed themselves. None of them is out to win a popularity contest; but each is fighting to preserve his or her humanity.

The most significant difference between my first book of monologues and the current offering is the recurrent motif of fatherhood that colors almost every page. Even though it was a percolating desire since I was a kid, I never expected to experience the role of being a dad. As a single, gay, HIV-positive man on the other side of forty, the likelihood of my being able to adopt seemed nearly impossible.

Only when I reviewed the pieces that appear in this book did I realize how parenthood has affected my art. Since the publication of *T-Cells*, I have evolved from capturing the voices of boys to the voices of men, from the voices of sons to the voices of fathers.

Many of *Life Expectancies'* inhabitants—from the autobiographical opening monologue from *Attachments* to the final war arias—probe the exhilarating and exasperating adjustments one faces when assuming the role of a father. Virtually nothing about being a parent is as one expects it to be, neither the agonies nor the ecstasies.

My daughter, Tia Katherine Kearns, is a fantastic gift, who has given me and my life, on and off the stage, a degree of passion I could never have imagined was attainable.

I dedicate the book to her and others like her whose difference is emblematic of their degree of empathy and beauty. I also dedicate *Life Expectancies* to my father, Joseph Kearns, who did the best he could but was never able to conquer his demons long enough to become the father I needed. I forgive him and honor him for providing me with the fuel to become an artist.

ATTACHMENTS

Michael

Michael is a gay man in his late forties.

My father, 1960; my roommate, 1994. A threadbare ter-
rycloth bathrobe, listless from too many spin cycles, hugs his
shuddering shoulders. When he aimlessly staggers from room
to room, as if not remembering the layout of the house, his
body appears to be in danger of caving in on itself, like a
defenseless building teetering on a hillside during a natural
disaster. He shuffles shamefully, like a man twice his age, never
lifting his swollen feet, tattooed with constellations of red and
purple splotches. He stares into nothingness as if a hidden
hint might float by, reminding him of who he was and what
exactly happened. With no such clues forthcoming, he shuts
his eyes, escaping into an unconscious void. When he makes
sounds, they are involuntary fart-like expulsions of excruciat-
ing pain, often merely a reminder—to himself, perhaps—he's
still alive. Sounds of night are less polite: volcanic eruptions
from the bowels of helplessness, like the pleas of trapped fire
victims. Is he waking from a nightmare? Or waking up to real-
ity? Only occasionally the sound of laughter is heard: a manic
giggle, signally something horrific, not something humorous.
The only time an expression of pleasure flickers across the
crevices of his corroded countenance is when he devours a cig-
arette. With each inhalation, he seems to recapture an evanes-
cent spark of his former self: a faint smile, a lithe movement of
the head. He sleeps more hours of the days than not, his disdain for light and dark indistinguishable. The doctors "don't
know" what's wrong with him—an undiagnosis that fuels his
indignant immobility. The terror of living compounded by
the terror of dying equals existence in a stagnant limbo. There

are days when my pity for him escalates to totemic hatred; if-only-he'd-die, I mutter to myself. On other days, my heart ricochets at the thought of losing him; we are inextricably entangled by a decade of life's highest dosage of drama. His presence makes me feel absolutely responsible, as if I'm the puppeteer who pulled the strings which have rendered him lifeless and impotent. And there's no question: if he dies, my mortality will zoom into focus. I vow not to be like him—a promise I relentlessly whisper to myself, determined not to wake the part of me that I know is him. My father, 1960; my roommate, 1994.

WHO'S AFRAID OF
EDWARD ALBEE?

George

George is the counterpart to George in the Albee play: intellectual but not without passion.

I was a teenager. Not even out of high school. It was the typical raging hormones/first love horniness scenario. She got pregnant—my first girlfriend. Her parents were these devout Catholics who did not believe in abortion. Marriage was not an option. So it was decided that she would carry the baby to full term and put it up for adoption. My feelings, what I wanted, weren't even considered—even though that baby she was carrying was mine, my flesh and blood. The more pregnant she became, with each pound she gained, the more guilty I became. Guilty and angry and horny. I wanted to rip that baby out of her stomach and claim it as my own. I wanted to fuck her until she gave birth. I wanted to mutilate her parents. But, instead, I became passive, immobile, paralyzed, inert. In nine months' time, I went from being a rowdy, raucous boy to a somber, sober man. A few weeks before she was due to deliver, mom and dad took their daughter to an undisclosed location where she gave birth to my child, my son, my daughter (I never knew which). The baby was immediately put up for adoption. I took responsibility for every pregnant woman I encountered. They were my children in their protruding bellies. I was responsible. Yet I could not have one of them. I could not touch. Or hold. Or say, "I love you." Or play in the park. Or teach them to ride a bike. For the next twenty-five years, I studied the faces of every child, every teenager, every young adult who would show up in my life, thinking maybe this is the one. When I found out Josie was pregnant, instead of feeling joy, it was revived horror, shame, guilt. The baby growing inside Josie's stomach became inter-changeable with the child I'd never seen. I felt unworthy of being a father, a husband. This is my secret. I withdrew, retreated; I shrank. I could not touch her, touch it.

TELL-TALE KISSES

Mick/Nick

Mick/Nick is a born-again, former gay, in his twenties.

What would you do if you could go from feeling like a sissy to feeling like Superman? From shame to pride? What would you do if you could go from feeling like an ugly duckling to feeling like fashion model on a Sunset Strip billboard? From frightened to brave? What would you do if you could go from feeling like a total flop to feeling like a box office star? From a nobody piece of shit to a somebody piece of flesh? You'd do it, wouldn'tcha? I did—like magic. Crystal. The Doctor turned me on to crystal, shortly after I arrived in L.A.—almost ten years ago. He wasn't like any doctor I'd ever seen—except maybe George Clooney. He was an AIDS doctor with style. You know, house in the Hollywood Hills, personal assistant, personal trainer, personal masseur. And I, after one meeting at a bar in West Hollywood, became his personal fuck. And fuck we did. High on crystal. For hours, days, seemingly weeks on end. I can't tell you the number of appointments he cancelled. Fucking me seemed to take precedence—for a while, anyway. Never, by the way, with a rubber. "The AMA makes us get tested every six months," he told me. "I'm negative and plan to stay that way." Seemed okay to me—I'd never really been fucked before and believe me, the crystal helped. The crystal helped everything. Made me transform. In fact, I only felt like me when I was high— the me I always wanted to be. The Doctor cured what ailed me—even though some of his patients were dropping like flies. We were together about a year. Vacations, circuit parties, dinner parties, orgies. I lasted longer than the personal assistant, the personal trainer, and the personal masseur. During that year, he taught me a lot—how to speak right, how to order in a restaurant, how to dress, how to make myself presentable. He changed my name from Mick to Nick; "Nick is tougher, more balls," he said. He might have turned me into a drug addict but I was a drug addict who had it together. When I came to L.A., I didn't know a thing—all I knew is that I couldn't be gay in a small town in the Midwest. My parents would have kicked me out if they ever found out, so I just left. The minute I graduated from high school. I don't think my parents noticed; it was probably a relief to them. They knew there was something wrong with me, knew I was different. They were pretty religious types and being gay was not okay; they expected me to get married and raise a family. The Doctor rescued me, in a way. At least that's what I thought at the time. After my nineteenth birthday—that's when he gave me this elaborate tattoo on my butt—I knew my days were numbered. It was like he marked me for life with that tattoo and he was finished. He got bored with everyone, always expected more. More of everything. More sex, more drugs, more money, more fame. He was more like a celebrity than a doctor. I never understood why a doctor would put his picture in a newspaper advertisement, but he did—looking like a soap opera star. When a new personal fuck arrived in town, I was history. Out on the street. He gave me 500 lousy bucks, not enough to rent an apartment. I used it to score some drugs and get laid. What else? Getting laid, high on crystal, was all I knew, really. And I knew I needed to make money to keep it up. So I began turning tricks. And dealing drugs. Sex and crystal, crystal and sex. I sold both—sometimes to the same person. Some of the Doctor's fancy-schmancy friends. It came as no big surprise to me when I found out the Doctor was dying. That sonofabitch wasn't HIV-negative. When I told somebody that doctors were required to be tested every six months, they laughed in my face. I guess my becoming positive was inevitable, a part of being gay. Being a party boy in L.A.

Comes with the territory. And, the truth is that it's not as big a deal as it used to be. Guys my age probably aren't gonna die from AIDS. There's a cure coming down any minute. Thank God for me since I really am in the midst of a major change. Things got pretty bad. I met this one guy who'd lost his lover—died in his arms, after being together for eleven years. When he found out I was positive, he began paying me to fuck him without a rubber. Once, twice a week; then three times, sometimes four. He'd try to time it so we came simultaneously. When he came, at the exact moment I came inside him, he told me that he thought about his dead lover. He thought about them being together again. With every fuck— every $65 check he'd write me—he was closer to being reunited with the love of his life. He believed it, and so did I, I guess. It made it hotter for me if I believed he was gonna meet up with this guy he'd spent most of his life with, this guy he loved so madly. He'd say his name as he exploded all over his belly and I shot inside him. "Steve. Steeeeeve," he'd scream. Sometimes "Steeeeevieeeee." And then he'd usually cry. Sob. In my arms. Then he'd get up and write me a check. And I'd go buy some more crystal. Truth is, I got tired of all the sex and drugs, endless partying, relentless hangovers. Never enough. Always needed more. Really strung out. At one point, I even tried to connect with my parents. Told them I was gay and they told me to never call them again. Unless, of course, I changed. I met Pete at this coffee shop on Santa Monica Boulevard. East of Fairfax, not my usual beat. He was this middle-aged guy, probably about the same age as my father, who didn't look like he lived in L.A. He was not the least bit glamorous (even old queens in L.A. try to pull it together). Turned out, he wasn't a queen at all. Asked me if I'd like to have coffee. God knows I wasn't attracted to him, but I said yes. And he told me his story. He was, he said, an "ex-gay." He had undergone a transformation and was letting people, like me, know it was possible. Ex-gay. At first, I didn't like the sound of it. I'd worked so hard to be the gayest of gay—the body, the drugs, the attitude, the clothes. The more he talked, the more I listened. He said he could sense certain things about me. And he was right. He could tell I was unhappy being gay; he could really feel my pain. He knew I was sick of selling my body, sick of the drugs, sick of the lifestyle. I probably wasn't really gay, he said. It was just something I got caught up in. Maybe he was right, I thought to myself that first night. We must have talked for a couple of hours. After the coffee shop closed, we sat his car and talked. It didn't seem strange when he put his hand on my leg—it was like a dad or an older brother. He said he had this feeling we were destined to meet; I was put in the coffee shop for a reason, he was certain of that. He took me to this apartment where I'd been crashing and gave me his card with a number to call if I decided I wanted to change my life. To become an ex-gay, like him. "It is possible," he promised. And it is. Pete took me to all these meetings. Not only did I have to stop having sex with guys, I had to rely on God to get me off drugs. Prayer would have to replace all my evil behavior. If I wanted to stay alive, I had to stay clean; stay off drugs and stay away from the gay lifestyle. It wasn't easy. First, I had to detox. Thank God for Pete; he was always there for me, like some kind of an earth angel, holding my hand. I came to believe that maybe I wasn't gay, after all. It was probably the drugs' fault. Without the crystal for a couple of months, I was beginning to see the light. The light of normality. I prayed and went to meetings, went to meetings and prayed. I turned my life over to the ministry. I didn't hate other gays, I felt sorry for them. Instead of thinking about depraved sex with men, I began thinking about marriage and children. Before too long, according to Pete, they're gonna be able to spin the HIV out of semen so that heterosexuals who are positive will be able to have kids. It'll be as simple as having a tattoo removed (which I did, last week—Pete, God love him, paid for it). When I get the virus out of me, there will be nothing homosexual about me. Pete says I have to stay clean for an entire year. Or more if necessary. A lot of guys go out and never come back. They lose themselves real fast. I'm becoming my true self. My parents said I could come home now that I've come to my senses. When I'm certain I'm healed, I'm going to go home to Indiana and raise a family. There was one fall—that's what the ministry calls a slip, when you fall off your path of abstinence. A kiss. This other guy—boy? man?—and I were praying together one night, praying to remain clean, praying to change. I don't know how it started, or who started it; it just seemed to happen so unexpectedly, so naturally. One minute we were praying and the next minute we were kissing, kissing with all our might, kissing with the same passion we had been praying with. Louis. As in St. Louis. It was my first sober kiss, unfucked-up on drugs. Maybe that's why it seemed sweeter and softer than all the other man kisses. It was distinctly different. Maybe it was because we were united in this quest to change; maybe that's what made it seem so much more—what's the word?—truthful. After it was over, we promised each other it wouldn't happen again. Even though we didn't go any further, it was too tempting. Like a hopeless alcoholic trying to drink only wine, it wouldn't work; just kissing wouldn't be permissible. I didn't tell Pete. That kiss. Louis. It haunts me. True to our promise, we never kissed again. Louis killed himself. He left a note saying it was better to be dead than to be a homosexual; God would accept him dead. He went home to his parents, got his father's gun, and shot himself. They found him splattered all over the garage. From the moment I heard he was dead, I could taste him inside my mouth. And that taste hasn't gone away. It's a strange sensation—like blood and sugar mixed together on my tongue. It's definitely Louis. I haven't had a fall since Louis. But sometimes I dream about him. The same dream. Not sometimes, all the time. And we're not even touching in the dream. We're separated by bars—like in a jail—and we're both naked. Masturbating. Staring into each other's eyes. Once, after coming in my sleep without touching myself, I woke up, screaming his name: "Louis." The sound of my voice woke me up: "Louis." I had that taste in my mouth. Dark and sweet. His permanent aftertaste. (*Screaming*) Looooouiiiiis.

Helen

Helen, late forties, is a true survivor who refuses to give up hope in spite of his travails.

Good news, bad news: alive, blind. Thanks to the drug cocktails, I'm as perky as a poodle in heat. But because of the CMV—supercalifragilistc-cytomegalovirus—I'm as blind as a bat. Blind as a batwoman, my friend Jamey says. He likes telling people I metamorphosed from Helen Lawson into Helen Keller practically overnight. It was kinda like Bette Davis in *Dark Victory*—only I wasn't planting bulbs, darlin', I was cruising Griffith Park. Even though I could still feel the sunshine beating on my bare midriff, it seemed to be getting dark awfully early. I hadn't even nabbed a single trick. By the time I got in my car, it was virtually impossible to drive. I'm fairly certain it's the first 911 call from an AIDS-stricken queen in Griffith Park, dialing from her cell phone: "Help me, honey, I think I'm going blind." Come to think of it, I probably sounded a bit like Bette Davis: "Help me, honey, I think I'm going blind." For those of you who don't know, Helen Lawson was the Broadway star in *Valley of the Dolls* who has a delicious bitch fight with Neely O'Hara, played by Patty Duke. Patty, of course, played my new alter ego in *The Miracle Worker*. If you don't know who Bette Davis is, you probably won't understand another word I say. Anyway, since Jamey calls me "Helen," I've taken to calling her "Annie." As in Annie Sullivan played by Anne Bancroft, not the-sun-will-come-out-tomorrow Annie. Jamey and I are decidedly influenced by the movies—like so many queens. Growing up in the south, we were lucky to find each other—at a movie theatre in Knoxville, where else?—watching Audrey Hepburn in *My Fair Lady.* Two sissy teenagers and a buncha white trash housewives dreaming of finding our own Henry Higgins. Jamey and I bonded immediately and promised each other we'd escape Tennessee the minute we graduated from high school. We decided we'd to go—where else? Hollywood— since both of us knew we were destined to be involved in show business. We arrived in L.A. in 1972. As it turned out, Jamey found his Henry Higgins almost immediately—in a leather bar on Melrose—and migrated to San Francisco where he pursued a theatre career—actor, director, producer—until he retired a few years ago. Jamey's marriage to Master Henry, as I called him, lasted longer than either of us expected. They were a notorious couple during all of the '70s—especially in the glamorous world of leather queens. I, in the meantime, got into hair and makeup in Hollywood: a career I'd been training for my entire life. For a time there, I was in demand. Cher, Ann-Margret, Goldie, the Divine Miss M—I did 'em all. Bette used to say, "You're my eyes, honey." Her eyes. I always managed to find time to visit Jamey and Henry in S.F.—in fact, I don't think I missed a summer season. I refuse to drone on about the seventies, but it was something, honey, something spectacular. And nowhere was it more sexual, sensual, or spiritual than in San Francisco. We were constantly connecting—mouth to mouth, soul to soul, dick to dick, skin to skin, heart to heart—with all our considerable might. From Folsom to the Castro, we fucked and cocksucked ourselves into a zany frenzy: connecting, connecting, connecting after so many years of being cut off, shut out, shit on, turned in. We were free. Then in the eighties; instead of bathhouses, we started attending support group meetings. HIV-this, HIV-that. Jamey took care of Master Henry—even though they'd been divorced for several years—when he got sick in 1984. Or was in '85? It all blurs. My visits to San Francisco were a bit less fevered, but no less revered. There was an energy there which was all inclusive—people with AIDS were safer than anywhere in the world. I remember going to the Castro

Theatre with Jamey to see *Magnificent Obsession*—the one
with Jane Wyman, not Greer Garson. In case you don't
remember, the character played by none-other-than Rock
Hudson accidentally hits Jane in a car accident. She becomes
blind—as a batwoman—and he determinedly becomes an eye
surgeon in order to restore her sight. At the time, Jamey and I,
and probably most of the people in the Castro Theatre that
night, saw it as an AIDS metaphor—especially with Hudson
as the leading man. Imagine being saved by the gorgeous
hunk who caused your suffering. Little did we know, as we sat
in that theatre, that I would one day be as blind as Jane
Wyman. After seeing the movie, Jamey told me this story
about his grandmother: He was in a high school production
of *Harvey*, playing the Jimmy Stewart role. His grandmother,
in her eighties, was in the audience when there was a power
outage. Everything on stage went pitch black. All Jamey could
hear was his elderly grandmother screaming at the top of her
lungs, "I'm blind. I've gone bliiiiiiiind." I'd have him tell me
that story whenever I got depressed—it made me howl. The
story is still funny although I don't request it as often these
days. Truth is, Jamey and I can't believe we've lived more than
halfway through the nineties. I tested positive in 1987—merely a confirmation of what I'd already assumed. My work had
dropped off—a lot of those broads became afraid to have their
faces touched by a fag. No, I'm not kidding. They'd get their
hair and makeup done—by some hetero stylist—and then
sashay off to an AIDS benefit. By the time things started getting better, I was yesterday's mashed potatoes. Thank God a
few of my regulars remained faithful. Jamey was one of the
first to be tested in S.F. and happens to be the only survivor of
that initial study he was involved in. He feels like a bit of a
dinosaur, in fact—"Katharine Hepburn of the Castro," he
calls himself. He recently told me he's decided to "own his
trollness." I visited Jamey a few weeks ago. Have cane, will
travel. He's not doing too well; the drugs ain't workin' and he's
virtually without an immune system. No energy, skin erup-

tions, depression, intestinal distress: the doctors call those "side effects." "If these are the 'side effects,'" Jamey says, "spare me the main event!" Any month, any week, any day, any hour—something could take hold and not let go. It's important we see each other as much as possible. Well, he sees me, anyway. I experience him. Jamey says I'm lucky I don't have to see what's happened to the Castro. "The Queens of Camouflage," he calls them. Stuffed with steroids, pumped up with protease, they are the nineties clones: muscled, pierced, tattooed, shaved. With "no detectable virus"—the battle cry of the healthy HIV-boys. It makes Jamey insane. "The Castro used to be a safe place for people with HIV," he shouts. "Now it's only safe if you're buffed, have more than 500 t-cells and no viral load." Jamey is pissed off at what he sees; I'm pissed off at what I can't see. I can't imagine what they thought of me and Annie Sullivan stumbling around, holding onto each other for dear life. "Helen," Jamey said, "You don't want to see their deadly looks of disdain." We persevered, referring to ourselves as "The Bland Leading the Blind." Jamey and I spend most of our time reminiscing: Remember the time . . . ? Remember the day . . . ? Remember the guy . . . ? Remember the party . . . ? Remember the bar . . . ? Remember, remember, remember. In my memory, I can see: I can see the colors of every gay pride parade; I can see holidays and birthdays and memorials; I can see the faces of every man I ever kissed; I can see all of my past but none of my present. Mostly Jamey and I try to remember who died when. Did David die before Joe? Was it '89 or '90? Was Jim before or after Chesley? Which Jim? Did you visit him in the hospital? Was Sam in '93? Has it been five years since Philip? Or is it six? Like old ladies in a nursing home, we hold on to these clues which define our past, the history that binds us. If Jamey dies before me, I'll have no one to confer with on our death data. Like my sight, part of me will be lost. How much more can I lose before I simply don't exist? During my recent visit, Jamey insisted we were going to have a fab Saturday night. "Like the good ole days," he said. "Is there a sock hop at the local Braille Institute?" I asked. "It's a surprise," he said. I told him, "I need a surprise like I need a new pair of opera glasses." Thank God I didn't have to see what I was wearing. Jamey dressed me—at least I couldn't feel any tassels or feathers. He also did my hair. Now he was my Henry Higgins. And I was Audrey Hepburn. In *Wait Until Dark*. And when it was dark enough, we headed for our destination: a sex club. I could smell sex before we opened the door to the place. If a blind Al Pacino could dance the tango, I figured I could suck a dick or two. "It's cool," Jamey assured me. "These guys are friendly—the old guard San Francisco queers." For those of you who've never experienced the joy of a glory hole, a history lesson. They used to exist primarily in public bathrooms— a hole about this size (*Indicates an oversized one*) to accommodate an erect penis. Wishful thinking, darlin'. Before we were liberated, this was a common way to get, or receive, a blowjob. In the fifties and sixties, anonymity was one of the lures. Of course, if you were bold, you might peek at your partner but it was probably wiser to fantasize he looked like Tab Hunter or Rock Hudson. Since many queers had their first sexual experiences on one end or the other of a glory hole, we continued to eroticize the experiences. Places like Blow Buddies—(no, I'm not kidding)—the club Jamey so graciously escorted me to, had these little cubicles—think confessionals, if you're Catholic—complete with perfectly drilled holes. Never in my life could I imagine how some queens managed to drill glory holes in the johns at Bloomingdale's. But they did, honey, they did. So anyway, Jamey led me into one of the closetlike spaces, complete with a lock on the door to secure my safety. "I'll check on you in a bit, Helen," he promised, slithering off to the room with slings. For the next hour or so, it didn't matter that I was blind. Or old. Or skinny. Or HIV-positive. All that mattered was my ability to get their horny rocks off. One after another, I fondled and licked and sucked and swallowed while they grunted and groaned and moaned and wallowed. No two dicks are alike, honey: cut, uncut, cucumber fat, pencil thin, long and graceful, short and stubby. In fact, each cock has it own personality: some are buoyant, others are tired, some guys gush, others dribble; some are obviously attached to men, others to boys. I was admittedly getting a bit tired, maybe delirious, when I thought I heard this guy in the adjoining booth say, "Let's kiss." Great, I thought to myself, now there's something wrong with my hearing. He couldn't have said, "Let's kiss." Too many late-night movies. "Huh?" I said. "Kiss me," he said, loudly, speaking into the glory hole as if it was a megaphone. Suddenly, before you could say "romance novel," I was kissing the boy-next-door-stranger, as if my life depended on it. And maybe it did. His kiss, like Prince Charming's, awakened something in me that I thought was dead; resurrected something I needed in order to keep going. I never thought I'd ever be kissed by a man again. But here I was, Miss Damaged Goods, being mouth-to-mouth resuscitated by a man who wasn't making any judgments. And kissing him, I could see; my bleak blackness was brightened by the glow of his soul, the heat of his heart, the light of his insides. A kaleidoscopic kiss, lasting for what seemed like hours but was too, too short. And of course it's what I needed—the thrill of a man's mouth on mine; the marriage of his tongue melded to mine; the taste, the smell, the sound, the feel of a ravishing kiss. Jamey couldn't get over it. "Sounds like you found your magnificent obsession," he said. "It's true," I agreed. He may not have restored my sight but he restored me. My hope. My belief in the goodness of queer men. Only Jamey could really understand. And who will remind me of that night if Jamey dies? Who? Did it really happen? Or did I make up my magnificent obsession? I've always been good at make up. What next, darlin'? Dementia?

Roger

Roger is a gay man with both a son and a lover dying.

If I've learned anything in my sixty-seven years on the planet Earth, it's this: with every accelerated heartbeat, there is an accompanying heartache; to love is to lose; to lose is to transform. I married Janet, my childhood sweetheart, in 1950. We were both only nineteen, barely out of high school. Even though our respective parents were decidedly middle-class, our marriage was prearranged, as if we were royalty. Friends since childhood, everyone knew Roger and Janet would one day marry. What they didn't know is that we would not live, like fairy tales dictate, happily ever after. I, of course, always knew. Even though Janet and I had a picket-fence existence—including a bouncing boy, born almost nine months to the day after our marriage—I knew. I knew I was living an all-consuming lie that would—if ever I was caught—both libel me and liberate me. I loved Janet, yes, the way you love the familiar. I did not love her the way a man loves his wife. For a while, Roger Jr. made my secret worth keeping. Being a dad was the only role I knew how to play; at no time did I feel more human or more alive than I did with my boy. I could not jeopardize losing my son. But after a few years, I knew I was jeopardizing the loss of my self; how could I be a good father if I was not my self? After graduating from the local Washington University, I got a job teaching music in my hometown of St. Louis. Music, in fact, provided my sanity, my passion, my connection to a world outside of myself. Coward, Porter, Gershwin, Hammerstein, Hart: the lyrics of those masters, laced with longing, became more real to me than my day-to-day disguise. By the time Roger Jr. was no longer a toddler, I had begun a dangerous dance, finding excuses to get away from the house. During summers, I'd go to the St. Louis Municipal Opera to escape in musical comedies: *The King and I, Take Me Along, Bells Are Ringing.* I'd often sit in the free seats that seemed about a mile from the stage. It was there that my life was forever changed. I saw him looking at me from a distance; his black bushy moustache set him apart from the crowd. His smile made me sweat; his heat was greater than any summer night I'd ever experienced. Even though the show was about to begin, I found myself following him into the restroom. He was wearing tight, hot, white pants, starched like a sailor's, an invitation to lust. From afar, I could hear the overture beginning as his hands pulled my face towards his. This was not the first time I brushed up against a man in a public bathroom but I'd never been romanced by one. I'd never heard a man say the words, "Kiss me"; I'd never tasted a man's tongue; I'd never felt a man's moustache scrape against my lips; I'd never smelled a man's sweat mixing with mine; I'd never seen a man's eyes penetrating me. We were arrested. Vice officers had taken photos of our luxurious kiss through a skylight window. We were thrown in jail, called the usual names. How many of you had your first queer kiss reported in the local paper? My job was over, my marriage was over, my relationship with my parents was over. And most damaging of all, I was no longer able to be a father to my son. Janet blamed herself; if only she'd been more like Donna Reed, she felt. Even though she took on the responsibility of turning me into a queer, she couldn't forgive me. After a lifelong friendship, I became her loathed enemy. She refused to let me see my son. And even my own parents supported her. After a period of prolonged guilt and humiliation, she finally killed herself, leaving Roger Jr. parentless. Although I pleaded to gain custody of my son after her death, there was no contest. How could a cocksucker raise a child without a wife? What could I do but flee? It wasn't being known as a fag that drove me away. It wasn't the rejection of my parents and friends. It wasn't Janet's suicide. It wasn't even the loss of my job. It was the pain of being unable to connect with my boy, knowing he was nearby but impossibly far away. I couldn't take the constant ache of it. In 1956, the only place in the world I might find some acceptance was New York City. And there was the lure of music: nightclubs, the Broadway stage, opera, jazz, symphonies. Not to mention the men who made music. In fact, I met Harvey at the opening of *My Fair Lady*—only a few days after I arrived in the city. Even though the particulars were dramatic, I was not unlike many other young men arriving in New York in the mid-fifties in search of self. I had no idea who or what I was—other than the father of a son I would probably never see and a man who hungered to be kissed by other men. Harvey changed all that. We were both in the standing room section of the theatre where many single, out-of-work men watched shows. Harvey was a budding composer with an incredible ear. "You sound like you're from the Midwest," he guessed, during the intermission, doing what I thought was a Henry Higgins parody. Then he surprised me: "St. Louis to be exact!" Funny. It was a foreshadowing of our relationship; although he was only a few years older, he did become my mentor. And my lover. In fact, other than the man at the Muny Opera in St. Louis, Harvey is the only man I've ever kissed. In many ways, he replaced the father who had never really been a father; even before my debut as a public pervert, my father must have sensed my queerness and kept his distance. Harvey and I have been together now for more than forty years. As together as life allows. In less than a year's time, I lost my son but gained a life partner. And although the joyousness of making music with Harvey, on and off the stage, was a reason to celebrate every day, there was a gouge in my heart that never mended. As each year passed, as my relationship with Harvey cemented, my longing for Roger Jr. escalated. I'd imagine what he looked like—at 10, at 15, at 20, at every holiday, at every birthday, every single time I saw a father and his son. There was one occasion in the mid-seventies, a time when New York was bursting with handsome young men, I swore I spotted him in a restaurant in the Village. Harvey and I had celebrated our twentieth anniversary at the Cafe Carlyle—with Bobby Short at the piano—and we were ravenous. In those days, it was not unlike us to be eating supper as the sun was about to come up. As we sat down at our table, a young man who looked exactly like I did on my wedding day, walked by our table. Even Harvey could see the resemblance. It couldn't be, could it? Nearly twenty years passed before I found out that it probably was Roger Jr. in that Greenwich Village all-night restaurant. He contacted me a couple of years ago with the proverbial good news, bad news: I want to see you; I have AIDS. Over the telephone, he explained how he needed to find some peace before he died. He needed to know who his father was. I told him that my needs were similar. Even though he was in his forties, he was devastatingly handsome. And, yes, gay. A writer of some accomplishment who had assumed the surname of his adoptive parents. I'd even read some of his political commentary in the gay press. He was doing well on the drug cocktails when our lives intersected a couple of years ago. We didn't go on *Oprah* (although we could have, God knows) but ours was a tearful reunion, riddled with equal measures of rejoicing and regretting. We attempted to celebrate forty Thanksgivings, forty Christmases, forty Easters, forty Fourth of Julys. Perhaps my greatest sadness was that I couldn't share this momentous event with Harvey. The other great love of my life had been deteriorating from the ravages of Alzheimer's for several years when Roger Jr. appeared. Not only was Harvey unable to recognize my son, he was unable to recognize me. Fate, I suppose, had determined that I could never have both of them, my son and my lover, at the same time. Not a day had gone by—since that night we stood watching *My Fair Lady*—that I hadn't been with Harvey. And even though I was no longer able to care for him, I visited him on a daily basis—even though I could have been Eliza Doolittle herself for all he knew. Roger Jr. and I enjoyed each other's company—plays, concerts, even performance art. We spent many hours discussing the whys of our homosexuality, deciding it might simply have been a wonderful coincidence. He was, in spite of the disease that killed so many of his friends and lovers, a happy man. That's what a father desires most. The burgeoning love for my son was eclipsed only by the pain of losing my beloved Harvey. As each month passed, Harvey became less and less himself, more and more a stranger to his own body, like a man inhabiting the wrong house. If his soul was intact, it was incognito. When Roger Jr. began experiencing dizzy spells, it didn't seem like there was cause for alarm. His immune system was, all things considered, fairly strong and doctors seemed confident he could fight off almost anything. Almost. He can't fight PML, a particularly vicious manifestation of AIDS that renders one as helpless as an Alzheimer's victim. A rapid deterioration. Marked by blindness, paralysis, incontinence, and dementia. Roger Jr. is in the final stages; like Harvey, he no longer knows me. I go from the hospice to the nursing home, back and forth, visiting the lost loves of my life, both of them disconnected, distanced, diseased. Who, I wonder, will die first? As I prepare for their deaths, I am already alone. It's not unhappiness I'm feeling, please believe me. It's an ecstasy tinged with horror; the spectacular sensation of love in all its transitoriness. Death will only provide these love stories with their final punctuation. In the meantime, I remind myself that I am a very lucky man.

COMPLICATIONS

Ronnie

Ronnie is a self-assured gay man in his fifties who doesn't shy away from being outrageous.

Jackie Kennedy. As a thirteen-year-old, little did I realize that she would prove to be my role model. Along with almost every single household in America, our family huddled in front of the television to experience the widow's star turn. This was far more exciting to me than John Glenn's trip to the moon the year before. We couldn't get enough of Jackie. I got to stay home from school the day after the President died, the day Jackie Kennedy became my beloved diva. Beautiful Jackie. Sad but beautiful. Jackie the perfect mommy. Jackie the bereaved wife. Jackie in black. Jackie in pain. Strong Jackie. Strong, strong, strong Jackie. No cheap soap opera theatrics, no ma'am. Jackie was almost Sphinx-like in her composure; someone must have given her that actress advisory—if you cry, the audience won't. Jackie made death glamorous. Death increased her ratings. Her popularity soared. My brother, disturbingly heterosexual, didn't pay much attention to Jackie—certainly not as much as me and my mom. But my brother's buddy, Allen, seemed to understand Jackie's allure. I remember the look on my brother's face when Allen described how the crimson bloodstains looked on her pink suit. He used that word: crimson. One day when he was waiting for my brother, he came into my room to see my Jackie photos, adorning every inch of my bedroom walls. Allen called it, "Jackie wallpaper." Jackie with Jack. Jackie with John-John. Jackie with Caroline. Jackie with Lyndon. Jackie on TV. Jackie on pain killers. Jackie laughing. But never, never ever Jackie crying. Allen loved her almost as much as I did. He eventually found excuses to visit when my tediously butch brother wasn't home, and one day, with Jackie looking on from all directions, we kissed. I imagine it was like the first time Jackie kissed Jack—so deep, so truthful, so romantic. Eventually, kissing led to cocksucking, with buttfucking not far behind. Jackie loved watching and we loved having her there. It was kinda like a three-way. My Neanderthal brother never found out. Allen chose to go to Vietnam. I think part of him looked at it as an escape from his fucked-up family and maybe part of him was trying to escape his homo feelings. Jackie and I missed him. I was in my senior year when it happened. I came home from school one day and saw my big, macho brother sitting on the front porch with his head buried in his hands. "Ah . . . Ah . . . Ah . . . Allen got killed." I could not cry. Remember Jackie. I touched my brother's shoulder (it's the only time I ever remember touching him, before or since), then opened the front door of our house, and with a studied calmness, walked to my room. "Hear the news?" my father asked, a bit blankly. "Yes," I whispered, sounding a bit too much like Jackie as I closed the door. They'll hear you sobbing, I said to myself. Look at Jackie. She did not cry. She had blood all over her pink Oleg Cassini—crimson blood—and she did not cry. I could not cry. Would not cry. Be strong. I am a widow now, a secret widow. Shortly after high school, I packed my Jackie photos and moved to Chicago where I went to school and where I would meet Joe. This was the early seventies when every gay man in America wanted to be Barbra Streisand but I remained faithful to Jackie—even though Joe made fun of me. Joe and I had a seventies marriage—three-ways, orgies, the baths. Poppers, Quaaludes, mushrooms. Oh, my. But it endured. Twelve years. And then Joe got this terrible flu. On about the fifth day, he was so sick that he had to go to the hospital. "He what?" I said, when the hospital called at about 3:00 A.M. "Died? He died? Joe died? Died? My Joe? He died? No, not my Joe. He's thirty-two years old. You don't die from the flu. You've made a mistake." I called a cab and arrived at the hospital about twenty minutes later. By the time I got there, the hospital had decided to call his parents and suggested I not complicate matters. They assumed Joe was closeted and they were right. "You probably shouldn't stay; it would just upset them. Their son is dead." "Yes, you motherfuckers, and my boyfriend is dead. My lover is dead. My husband is dead. My Jack Kennedy is dead," I wanted to say. Instead, I left, trying to remember how she carried herself as I walked—in Jackie's size eleven shoes, as it were—poised, head up, holding back all the accumulated tears. I vowed. Never. To. Fall. In. Love. Again. About five years later, I made a quilt panel for Joe. I had never even sewn on a button and suddenly I'm Betsy Ross on crack. I attached a photo of him, his favorite tie, and a letter he'd written me on our first anniversary, saying we'd be together forever. The Quilt was displayed at the March on Washington in 1987. Imagine me being in Washington, D.C., for the first time, visiting all the places where Jackie had been. I also decided to go to the Vietnam wall, to look for Allen's name. It was silent at the wall except for the sounds of sniffling. I found him: Allen Green. But I didn't cry. Not a single sniffle. I didn't even notice there was this handsome man standing next to me. "Excuse me," he said, as he stepped by me. Can you meet cute at the Vietnam wall? "Meeting cute" is a movie expression, describing the initial encounter of onscreen sweethearts destined to fall in love. Phil and I met cute at the Vietnam wall. He was there to look at his brother's name, and he also told me he was going to the opening ceremonies of the Quilt to see a panel he'd made for his dead partner. That's the word he used: "partner." We decided to meet early the next morning. Staring at Quilt panels honoring our dead lovers and dead partners and hundreds of our dead brothers, we fell in love. He lived in Minneapolis, and after about six months of a long distance romance, he moved to Chicago. He was an art historian and could pretty much work anywhere he wanted. Phil was all brains. It was an odd pairing. I was this overemotional drama queen and he was this cool, collected intellectual. We traveled all over the world and he taught me about art. All kinds of art—from the paintings of Van Gogh to the pyramids of Egypt. Our travels were fairly compulsive, like we were fighting to get everything in before we died, breathlessly inhaling every beautiful morsel within our reach. Phil started getting sick on one of our excursions. A vision thing that led to his eventual blindness. Imagine someone whose entire life was about using their eyes going blind. He died about ten years ago—in my arms. After my third foray as a widow, I vowed never to marry again. Liz Taylor I ain't. So I embarked on a journey of anonymous sex encounters, thinking I'd just burn out in a matter of months, but noooooooooo. Enter the three things that saved this girl's life: protease inhibitors, Viagra, and AOL. I actually met Randy online. His screen name was "singingflyboy." We began with the usual dirty computer chat and evolved (if you can call it that) to dirty phone sex. He had the sexiest voice; he was a singer who was moonlighting as a flight attendant. Singingflyboy. Get it? Since he worked for the airline, United, visiting in person was doable. I must say it was a shock the first time I saw him. He had never mentioned his ethnicity and it wasn't in his AOL profile. Well, Randy was black. I mean, black-black. Not cocoa, not cinnamon, not caramel. He was black, honey—as black as coal (and I don't mean Natalie), as black as night (and I don't mean Gladys), as black as a Halloween cat or a Hollywood limousine. We became fuck buds. During sex, he'd call me "daddy." If I was his daddy, his mommy must have been Butterfly McQueen. We probably got together a dozen or so times and it was always fine. That's a word he used a lot: "fine." In between visits, we were in constant touch by email. That's why I knew. I knew his schedule. I knew his flights. I knew he was on that Tuesday morning flight headed for San Francisco out of D.C. The flight that crashed in Pennsylvania, September 11, 2001. He'd given me a CD he recorded for friends—all flying songs. I'd never listened to it because I was afraid I wouldn't like it and what would I say? That CD was my inheritance. Ever listen to someone's answering machine after they died? This was even spookier: hearing him sing for the first time, alone in my apartment on September 11, as the muted television painted one tragic story after another. Of course, there was something from *Peter Pan,* "The Wind Beneath My Wings," and he actually wrote music to a scene from the movie *Airport* and sang the dialogue between Burt Lancaster and Maureen Stapleton. But my favorite was "Fly Me to the Moon." "Fly me to the moon and let me play among the stars. Let me see what spring is like on Jupiter and Mars." I just hope I know when to make my final exit. Timing is everything, honey. You don't believe Jackie died of natural causes now, do you? And consider what she managed to avoid: the death of her son, the Bush Administration, Liza's wedding. I'll hang in there—as long as I can get laid. Talk about irony; the very thing that will kill me is the very thing that's keeping me alive: Sex.

Carlos

Carlos is a scrappy, self-described "mutt" in his twenties; not without heart.

Simple-minded therapists say I'm searching for my real father. Seeking him in every sexual encounter, hoping to find him in every loada cum I take up my ass. Maybe it's his sperm I am in search of, the seed that bred me. That's what they say. I'm not so sure. True, my father is unknown. That's what it says on my birth certificate: "father: unknown." I'm a mutt. He musta been Latin. Maybe just plain old Mexican. Or maybe he was a mix. A splash of black, a dash of Asian. A pinch of nigger, a spoonful of gook. Who knows? Unknown. I don't know who the fuck I'm looking for but I do like those daddy types—their experience, their history, their strength. If you're a gay dude who's lived to be fifty, you must have something goin' on. Some kinda energy I want inside me: Daddycum. Wonder if my mother was searchin' for a father. She was a slut, that's for sure. It was my mother who taught me the art of being a power bottom. I'd watch her get plowed night after night—on her back, on her knees, on her stomach, on the floor, on drugs, on booze, on and on. And all of these suitors were potential hus-bands. Here's how it went: if they were there for only one night, she never introduced me to 'em, acted like those tricks didn't happen. If they stayed more than two nights, I was told to call the man of the house my "uncle." If Mr. Right hung around for a month or more, he was elevated to "dad." One of my "dads," in fact, seemed to like me as much as he liked mommy. After watching him fuck the shit out of her one night, he came into my room. I was fourteen. He didn't waste any time. Probably still dripping with mommy's juices, he just rammed it in me. This became routine. He'd fuck mommy, then fuck me. "Take it, son," he'd say. One night, mommy caught us—she flipped. It was, of course, my fault. How could I do this to her? Forget about the asshole with the unscrupulous prick. "You little bastard," she said. It was at this point she insisted we go visit the parish priest. Mommy was a devout Catholic. After a week of getting boinked by every Tom, Dick, and Harry, she'd spend Sunday in church, absolving her sins of the flesh. We went to Father Maloney who stared at me intently as Mommy told him that I obviously had "tendencies" and she was concerned. Perhaps the good father could speak to me alone, Mommy suggested. Confession might be appropriate. So I told him. The truth. "Bless me, father, for I have sinned." I believed it was my fault and especially my fault for likin' the feeling of jizz in my butt. You know what the fuckin' priest did? Didn't prescribe three Hail Marys and six Our Fathers. He told me that I made him hard—again, I was to blame—and eventually he wound up fucking me right there in the confessional. "My son," he muttered as he banged me against the flimsy wooden partition. "My son." After the priest finished, huffing and puffing like he was a cartoon character, he said, "Don't tell anyone, son." For not having a father, I had a lot of motherfuckers callin' me son. It was only a few weeks before mommy's paramour was back in my bed, pumping me with a load. I remember distinctly that the cum was a turn-on. You know why? When they came, that meant it was over. She caught us, for the second time, in the middle of the night, and like a wacko in a soap opera, she threw me out of the house. I didn't call Father Maloney. Luckily, I had a friend with these Bohemian-type parents who lived down the street. I was now fatherless, motherless, and homeless. They took me in. Pretty much let me do as I wanted. I started drinking, doing some drugs. And rarely went to school. I also started having sex with men—men who treated me better than the fake Dad and the fake Priest. I spent more and more nights in the homes of gay men than I did with the generous family. Even though she lived only blocks away, I never saw Mommy but as only people in small towns do, people began talking about her health. There was something drastically wrong, according to the gossip. Fate intervened and I ran into her at the Seven-Eleven. I almost didn't recognize her—painfully skinny with a gray skin color and she appeared to be perilously weak. She looked me in the eye. Her eyes were sunken. Even though I'm no medical authority, I'd seen enough images during my lifetime to know, unquestionably, Mommy had AIDS. No one—and especially Mommy—would dare say the word. This was a small town where AIDS didn't exist because queers and whores and drug users didn't exist. I would, if she'd let me, move in and take care of her. Until the end. Allowing me back in her life was not easy. That would be admitting she was sick. But eventually, she was too weak to fight me. I took care of her for a year or so, each day inching toward the inevitable. Although never officially diagnosed—because she was "in God's hands" and refused to go to a doctor—I was right about AIDS. She became completely withdrawn, allowing no one near her except me. I did what you do under the circumstances: bathed her, tried to keep the fevers down, changed her diapers, carried her from one room to the other when she could no longer walk, dressed her bed sores, brushed her teeth, combed her hair, fed her, cleaned up her vomit, and read her uplifting stories from the newspaper. One story stood out, a story I would not read to her. A story that did not uplift. It seems that a group of seven young men who lived in our town, men in their late twenties/early thirties, had become mysteriously ill. Mostly men with wives and kids. All identified as heterosexual. None was a drug user. Or a hemophiliac. Yet they all tested positive for HIV; two of them were severely ill. There was only one link that all these men shared: they were all Catholic. Each one of them had all attended Father Maloney's church. And—you guessed it—they had all been boinked by Father Maloney. And these men, on behalf of their wives and parents and children and brothers and sisters and all those who might lose them prematurely, were pursuing a lawsuit that named him, essentially, as their murderer. Sex—as often as possible, with as many men as possible—made the fear temporarily subside. She'd be in the other room, asleep, and I'd be getting fucked, night after night, trying to ease the pain, the ache, the emptiness, the relentless sadness. Is this what she was attempting to do when I was a kid? Were those men the anchors that kept her from going completely out of her mind with too many fucking feelings? How could I not forgive her? Days after I assured her that all was forgiven, she died. I had to move away if I was gonna get anywhere in this world. So I came to the Big City where there are AA meetings on every street corner. I'm getting my high school equivalency and working as a gardener. And still having way too much sex. There are these guys I do work for: Daniel and Corey. They both give me the eye, but for different reasons. When you are a mutt, a mixed-breed, you are regarded in a certain way. Either I'm exotic or I'm inferior, depending. Corey thinks I'm exotic. Daniel thinks I'm inferior. But it amounts to the same thing: they both want me. They've supposedly been in a monogamous/monotonous relationship for five years. Corey, the younger and hotter of the two, is usually at home when I'm doing the yard work so we became friendly. One day, he just kinda leapt on me and started kissing me. I was into it. I felt like I was in *The Young and the Restless* or some shit. This dude was starving for kisses. The kissing led to fucking—something else he never got from Daniel. At least that's what he said but these guys don't always tell the truth. So I kiss him and fuck him, fuck him and kiss him. Daniel was working late. We do it in the pool house, like it's a porn movie set. But with real moonlight. After I came, after I shot an unwrapped wad up his tight hole, he said, "You're clean, right?" "Yeah," I said. "I'm clean. I took a shower this morning."

Bo

Bo is a hot hustler on the other side of thirty.

I didn't always look like this. I was born in 1969: The year Barbra won the Best Actress Oscar for *Funny Girl*. The year we sent a man into outer space to walk on the moon. The year Judy Garland died and those brave queers, drag queens and leather boys among 'em, fought back at the Stonewall in Greenwich Village. Oh. And the year my dad was killed in Vietnam. Three weeks after I was born. So I guess you might also say that 1969 was the year my mom came very close to losing it. Very early on, it became apparent that she considered me indescribably delicate. Like a piece of glass. She was hysterically protective of me, virtually never letting me out of her sight. Was it her fear that made me a delicate kid or was her fear based on my being a delicate kid? Everything in her mind was potentially dangerous—cars, buses, the sun, the moon, neighbors, teachers. I was a kid and—even though I'd try to defy her at times—I knew she must be right. She was the authority in our house. Since I'd never seen my dad—only a few photos she'd shown me, none of them on view—I didn't really miss him. But I missed something. Some inexplicable yearning would manifest at the oddest times. I'd actually feel as if part of my body was gone—a leg, my head, my stomach. Being skinny didn't help. Maybe she didn't feed me properly for fear of certain foods but I was excruciatingly skinny. Make-fun-of skinny. I was convinced that part of me didn't exist. If I dare mentioned anything like this to her, she would shut me up and insist I was talking crazy. But I was in a state of constant aching. I decided maybe I was missing my father. But no, it was something deeper, something more mysterious. It was something I was convinced she was not telling me. Life changed dramatically when I was fourteen. That's when my mom took me to see *Yentl*—that movie where Barbra dresses like a boy. It was being shown with *Funny Girl,* which I had never seen. That's when I heard about a mysterious disease killing gay men and admitted to myself that I was gay. This was also the year—1983—when, for whatever reason, my Mom decided to tell me about my sister. My twin sister. The twin sister who had died in childbirth. Yes, my mother lost a baby and a husband within a month or so; I was the only one who remained. There is a photograph of my mother, obviously taken at my father's military funeral. She is carrying me, a month-old baby, in her arms with an American flag. The red, white, and blue fabric almost looks like a baby blanket. I have never seen my mother look so beautiful—it is that pure radiance possessed only by the stricken, as if the face is stripped of all pretense, leaving exquisitely raw emotion. (*As Barbra*) "Oh, my man I love him so . . ." Barbra. *Funny Girl.* Final credits. When she told me about my sister, my twin sister, the photo of my mother made even more sense. Her husband. One of her babies. Dead. She chose to wear masks from that day forward: the happy homemaker, the dutiful mommy, the good neighbor—forced false faces concealing any trace of real feelings. And she had been trying to protect me, I suppose, but finally I realized it was my sister I had been missing all this time; she was the source of my insatiable grief. Seeing *Funny Girl* did it. From the moment Barbra came on the screen as Fanny Brice, I was made whole again. (*Impersonating Barbra*) "Hello, Gorgeous." Barbra was my sister, I just knew it. I felt complete at last. And it was Barbra who would provide the blueprint for my life. Remember how gawky she was when she sang "I'm the Greatest Star"? That was me—skinny and geeky but full of unrealized potential. We were twins. Identical twins, Barbra and me. I don't know how many times I'd seen *Funny Girl* but by the time I graduated from high school, I knew every word of it. (*Impersonating Barbra*) "Mr. Ziegfeld, yoo hoo! Mr. Ziegfeld!" People would make fun of me but I didn't care; people made fun of Barbra, too. I finally moved away from my mother to go to college, leaving her totally alone. I couldn't fix her or heal her or sew up her shredded heart. I had to leave so that I could find my Flo Ziegfield and my Nicky Arnstein. Like Barbra, I would overcome my ugliness and become desirable. A man would see my beauty—and want me. It was a long process but I was patient and if ever I became fearful or questioning, I'd watch *Funny Girl*. Sometimes I'd avoid the sad ending and just concentrate on Barbra's triumphs. (*Impersonating Barbra*) "You plannin' to make advances?" I was having a lot of sex during this time, but with no one remotely resembling Nicky. And when you looked like I did—thin and creepy—I didn't insist on safe sex on the rare occasion I managed to get one in bed with me. I tested positive when I was thirty. All I could think of was my mom. She told me that there was a place for me to be buried next to my sister. How could she face another premature death? Of course, HIV is not really a death sentence anymore. In my case, in fact, it was the beginning of my transformation. Like Barbra's—from ugly duckling to swan. My doctor prescribed steroids to build up my weight. He was my Ziegfield in a way. I started going to the gym. And doing Human Growth Supplements. I knew I was on my way to desirability. A good haircut. The right clothes. It was all possible. They would love me. Like they loved Barbra—in spite of all the hateful past, I would finally be lovable. I eventually had so many Nickys, I didn't know what to do with them. Boyfriends who wanted me. I realized this hard-won allure of mine could be a commodity. Like Barbra's voice. I could sell myself. (*Impersonating Barbra*) "Some ain't got it, not a lump. I'm a great big clump of talent." I started turning tricks and it's been amazing. I feel like a star. The greatest star. I exist now. I have muscles. Star muscles. And men love me. You'd be surprised how many of 'em even wanna pay for my cum even knowin' that it's infected. If they're gonna get infected, it may as well be by a star. Right?

Mikey

Mikey, fortyish, is a drug dealer who is the sole caretaker for his mentally challenged brother.

I make about $5,000 a month, selling tina, and sometimes I treat myself to a big stud. I didn't think I'd grow up to be a drug dealer. I was Mr. Perfect. The perfect baby. The perfect toddler. The perfect teenager. The perfect gentleman. And I had perfect parents. With perfect careers and perfect cars. And we lived in a perfect house in a perfect neighborhood. And I was—you guessed it—the perfect son. When my brother came along, he would have a lot to live up to. Maxwell, also known as Max, also known as Maxie, was born when I was sixteen. Around the time I was achieving imperfection, coming out of the closet. From the beginning, Max was different. My parents began comparing him to me immediately. Max was not perfect. And from the moment I revealed my self, my true self, my gay self, to my parents, neither was I. All their bloated pride burst into a cyclone of profound disillusionment. They wanted to change me, offering to pay for therapy, whatever it would take to re-perfect me. Unlike some parents, they didn't blame themselves, they blamed me. "You have disgraced us." They could not hide their relief when I moved out of their house. Unfortunately for them, Max was not the perfect antidote. His behavior was atypical—even as a toddler, there were signs. And mommy and daddy were not pleased. Maxie was a temperamental kid—loud, silly, angry. Also incredibly affectionate and loving. When I would visit him (the only reason I came near my parents), he would cling to me, screaming my name over and over again. My father once said to me, "Don't touch him so

42

much," as if my faggotry would rub off. It was a preschool teacher who suggested Maxie undergo a battery of tests. If there was anything in my parents' mind worse than being gay, it was being diagnosed as developmentally disabled. Also known as retarded. Forget all the well-researched books, the cuddly TV *Movies of the Week,* the support groups—my parents would rather be dead than have a retard and a fag fall off the family tree. I don't really remember how it happened; it was inevitable. Maxie belonged with me, not with them. And they let go of him willingly. Our family split in two: the Perfects and the Imperfects. He's been living with me for the past six years. We divorced our parents. We have our own Thanksgiving, Christmas, Easter, and summer vacation. We don't need mommy and daddy on birthdays or Halloween or Valentine's Day. My baby brother can be a bit of a challenge. He spends some time at a special school but mostly he's at home with me. The school is fucking expensive—you can imagine. I needed to make a lot of money and not spend a lot of time doing it. A real job just didn't work. When the idea of selling drugs came up, it made sense. Oh. I should also mention that I tested positive for HIV about three years ago. Maxie and I had already established our imperfect family. It simply became more imperfect with HIV added to the mix. I began using crystal after testing positive. It seemed no more dangerous than all the other shit I have to pump into my body. The protease inhibitors. I use it during sex. It makes the experience even more of an escape. I don't get emotionally involved with the guys I fuck—crystal guarantees that. My emotions belong to Maxie. He owns my heart. I don't need a man to fulfill me. When Maxie is at school for an extended period of time, I do some crystal and have a big hot fling with a stranger. Then it's back to caring for my kid. And selling dope to dopes. I live in fear. Total fear. Fear I'll get caught selling. Fear he'll be taken away from me. He's my son, my buddy, my partner, my boy. I'm his daddy, his mommy, his teacher, his pal, his mate. We are a team. A pair. A twosome.

A pas de fuckin' deux. What really scares me—even more than the drug stuff—is the inevitable. I will get sick. I will, at some point, get sick. Oh yeah, I'm fine now but it's always present: the fear of death. What would he do without me? There are those stories you hear on the news about parents who kill their kids and then kill themselves. No one understands. They interview the neighbors. "How could she kill her own flesh and blood? She loooooooved those kids." The newscasters whine, "He was a devoted father. How could he kill those six boys, all under the age twelve?" We demonize them, label them evil. I'm sober at the moment, by the way, and I just wanna say that I understand. I understand what it's like to be so fucking scared of the future, of your kid's future without you. I understand. I'm not saying I'm going to do it. I'm not. But I get it: We're going to go on the ultimate vacation, the final trip. My kid, my angel, my soulmate, and me. Because I can't leave him behind. Because I don't want anyone else to take care of him. Because. He's. Mine. The other night we were driving home from the movies. It was very dark. And the moon was right in front of us; from the windshield, it seemed like we could drive into it. "It's low," Maxie said, in utter wonder. "And yellow." I told him he was right; it was low and yellow. And huge. "Go there, can we?" he asked. "To the moon together." I explained that it wasn't as close as it appeared. "But I'd very much like to go to the moon with you, Maxie," I said. Just the two of us. Moonstruck. Being together in space for eternity. He whispered (which he does infrequently), "I sleep with you tonight. We snuggle," sounding like a six-year-old instead of a soon-to-be adolescent. He only gets to sleep in my bed on special occasions. "Tonight big moon," he says. "Special 'cassion." "Yeah," I say, relieved that he's found a reason for us to lie close to each other. Brothers in love. In the glow of the moon. Special 'cassion. Do you believe the full moon makes people feel more intensely? Does it make you more horny? Gay men use it as an excuse to pig out and business is great.

So the phone began ringing off the hook on the night of the "big moon." Sometimes it's convenient to mix business with pleasure.

James

James is a weathered, beleaguered addict in his forties.

Forget, forget, forget. The crystal makes me forget. Forget the pain, put it on hold. As long as fucking possible. Try to remember, try to remember. My first experience with crystal was about a month after Gerald died. That was 1996. Now I have my own dealer. You do the math. Gerald was one of those guys who didn't catch the protease train. We had been together for almost ten years—steadfastly monogamous. He was poz, I was neg. He was older, I was younger. Him dying before me was a given, all things considered. But, no matter how much you think you're prepared, there is no preparation—no movie, no how-to book, no Oprah segment, that prepares you for the loss of a lover. I met him right after I got out of college. I had been with very few men—no more than a dozen or so. And nothing very adventurous. I was pretty leery of getting AIDS back then. So it was really astounding that I wound up marrying someone who was positive. I just couldn't resist him. Could. Not. Resist. Our relationship wasn't about sex; it wasn't typical in that way. No drugs, no three-ways, no sex toys. It was largely peaceful. And I suppose there were times when I thought I was missing out on something but as one year melded into the other, I became more and more secure that I made the right decision. Then he died and I started having lots of sex with lots of men. Maybe I felt I'd been depriving myself. Maybe I was angry—that's what my grief counselor said; my gluttonous sexual appetite was anger-based. Angry that Gerald died? Angry? No shit. The first guy who offered me crystal—I just could not resist. I was hooked almost immediately; the hours turned into days and days turned into weeks. Sex and crystal. Crystal and sex. Lost my job, lost my apartment, seroconverted, wound up in recovery. My whole life changed. Suddenly I was HIV-positive. Finally, I had an identity. I replaced sex and crystal with twelve-step meetings—AA, ACA, SCA, you name it—and put my anger in my back pocket, along with sex and drugs, and added celibacy to my identity. A celibate, HIV-positive man in recovery. The party invitations didn't exactly fill my mailbox. I actually believed that the best part of my life, life with Gerald, was over and I was just marking time until I died. I got my life back in order, including a new apartment and a new job—working as an assistant to a fashion photographer. I got to travel. That was nice. One trip took us to New York. After working all week, including most of Saturday, I decided to just roam around the Village, not expecting anything. I met Simon, standing in line at the Sullivan Street Playhouse, to buy tickets to see *The Fantasticks*. We met cute. I had never seen the show. "You're kidding," he said, truly nonplussed. "I have seen it once a year since I moved to New York almost twenty years ago." I had no idea it had been running twenty years. "Forty years," he said. I actually was standing in line to find out what time the show let out since I was supposed to meet some friends later that night for a late supper. Needless to say, I never met my friends. Simon and I saw *The Fantasticks*. We spent the next twenty-four hours together in some blissed-out state. Maybe it was because I was out of town; maybe that's why I let him in. Maybe it was *The Fantasticks*. Have you seen it? During the show, when something especially joyous or dramatic happens, they throw these little square-shaped tissues, made of all different colors, into the air. It's so cloyingly sweet and romantic. "*The Fantasticks* is my longest-running friend," he joked. If you can fall in love in a blink, we did. After the show and dinner at his favorite little Italian restaurant, we went to his apartment and made love for the next fifteen or sixteen hours. Our bodies fit inside each other; all the pent-up emotions were just flowing out of me and into him. It was fantastic. (I can't believe I said that: fantastic.) And then I was on a plane, coming back to the West Coast on the Sunday night/Monday morning red-eye. What did I even know about him? His obsession with *The Fantasticks* was the biggest clue to who he is. Mushy. Nostalgic. Kinda magical. Monday at work was a blur. Exhausted but exhilarated, I went home early, wondering who would make that first phone call. We had exchanged home phone numbers only. I figured I'd take a short nap. If he hadn't called by 6:30 or 7:00, I'd call him. I fell into a deep, deep sleep. The phone woke me up. It was 6:33. Tuesday morning. My friend Jim was fairly hysterical. "Turn on your television," he said. Still groggy, I hung up the phone and began grasping the fact that I was watching the collapse of the Twin Towers in New York City. The World Trade Center. Twin Towers. New York City. No, no, no. Simon did not say he worked at the World Trade Center. Twin Towers. No. I was dreaming that. Dreaming. I noticed my answering machine blinking. There was one message I'd obviously slept through. 10:07 P.M. "Hi, this is Simon," he said. "I think I'm in love." I began dialing his number but couldn't get through. I listened to the message he left, over and over. "I think I'm in love, I think I'm in love." I finally got through the next day. "Try to remember, the kind of September, when life was slow and oh so mellow." Then his voice, "Hey, this is Simon. Leave your name and number and I'll 'try to remember' to call you back." I called his number hundreds of times during the next few days as I watched the television, hoping for a clue. There were no clues forthcoming. I knew none of his friends, relatives, co-workers. On Friday, I received an envelope in the mail with his return address, postmarked September 11, 2001. I don't remember giving him my address. Try to remember. There was no letter inside. Only seven of those square-shaped tissues from the play: blue, pink, green, purple, yellow, red, orange. Even though I knew, I kept calling his number, listening to his

48

corny message, hoping to get a confirmation. At the end of September, a woman answered the phone. I didn't know what to say. So I hung up. It must have been a relative. The following day, the phone was disconnected. Dis-connected. I spend most of my time having sex and getting high. Dis-connected. You know those American flags that are fucking everywhere? I see his face on every one of them—on the car window in front of me, on the bag from the grocery store, flying high on top of buildings. I see that face of his superimposed on the red, white, and fucking blue. At one point, I thought about going to New York. See *The Fantasticks* again and find that Italian restaurant as a tribute. But one night I was in a stupor, watching television, and they said that the play had closed. Fuck. The fuckin' play died. I just wanna get laid, that's all. And forget. And get high. Don't remember, forget. Forget about him. Sometimes I take my pipe and sit in a room at the baths and wait for someone to come in.

Ralph

Ralph is a closeted black man who is living a double life.

"Daddy" made me think of my old man. My father's disapproval of me must have begun upon sight. Probably in the hospital room, almost immediately after I entered the world. Too dark, too much like my mama's side of the family. Upon sight: that's when he decided that I would have to compensate for being so dark, so black. Black-black. Too black. Way black. In his mind, I was destined to fail. His hope—that I would be like him: light-skinned and able to pass—was extinguished. Upon sight. He gave me his name, Ralph Watson Jr. The "Junior" was a constant threat, a challenge to live up to his accomplishments. What my father accomplished is a triumph of mendacity, a daredevil dance of deceit. My daddy learned this whitewashing trick from his daddy who, amazingly enough, was able to convince U.S. military officials during World War II that he was white. Because he did not want to be put in noncombat duty because of segregation rules, he deliberately used his lightness, enabling him to fight for his country. Along with other light-skinned black men, he loved America. Even though America didn't love them back. My father's motives were not so honorable. My dad decided to pass would make him a millionaire. He cashed in on the shade of his skin tone, as light as his heroic father's. He chose real estate, selling houses behind white picket fences in white neighborhoods to white people, letting them think he was white. In most instances, he considered my stunningly beautiful black mother a liability, essentially leading a double life. His world at home and his world at work rarely intersected. While a great disappointment for my father, my birth was a

50

great comfort for my mother who was quickly growing bitter and depressed living under such secretive circumstances. Growing up, it was my mother who instilled me with a sense of what it is to be black. But she did it cautiously, as if my self-acceptance might destroy the illusion my father had so painstakingly created. No roots in our house. The more money he amassed, the more I believe he actually thought he was white. Mama and I eventually left, surviving on our own terms. By the time I was a teenager, I hated him and his outlandish hypocrisy. I would not only be proud of my blackness, I would not only own my heritage, I would be vocal about it. And I wanted to, with all my heart; I wanted to attend rallies, make speeches, write articles. Yet I knew there was something that prevented me from being a positive role model, a black man who would be admired and respected. I was a black man who liked men. This was simply not acceptable. Gay white men may have found acceptance in the mainstream—in politics, the arts, even sports. But a black man? Who? Little Richard? Michael Jackson? I decided that I would not allow my feelings for other men to jeopardize my black pride. Would not, could not. I would silence those feelings. I would get married, have children. Prove my masculinity, insuring my image as a responsible black member of my community. Will Smith, Colin Powell, Magic Johnson: these are manly men. Yet, I could not stop having sex with men, secret sex with gay men. Could not, would not. White men only. I would not admit my gay shame to a brother. Could not, would not. Having sex with white men only complicated the shame. I was a traitor to both my blackness and my maleness. A wife and family would be the solution. I'd be able to stop. We got married. A beautiful black woman. When I attempted to make love to her, I re-created memories of sex scenes with white men, trying to make a black baby. I was a traitor to my race, to my masculinity. Most of the time, I have to fake it. I can not usually cum inside her. Cannot. I can barely stay hard. On the rare occasion I do ejaculate, it is shortly after sex with a man. The closer the memory of him shooting inside me, the more likely I can shoot inside my wife. The more sex with men, the more likely I'll get her pregnant.

Lisa

Lisa is a pregnant black woman whose successful exterior is threatened by her damaged interior life.

I spent my entire life rejecting the idea of having a family, being a wife and mother. Career came first. I refused to subjugate my potential catering to a man and to raising his children. I grew up in a household that taught me what not to be. My mother was the penultimate housewife and mother, an identity that consumed her. Nothing seemed to make her happier than cooking, cleaning, gardening, making clothes, decorating, baking—all while standing by her man. Even though my father was a blatant philanderer, my mother chose to look the other way while she repainted the bathroom for the umpteenth time. As a teenager growing up in the seventies, when my girlfriends' mothers were divorcing their no no-good husbands and venturing out into the world to pursue careers, my mother was an embarrassment. I went to a racially mixed school but hung out with mostly white girls. My mother's determined domesticity seemed so black to me, at a time when even some black women were refusing to be victimized. I so resented her. I tried to get her to read a book or a magazine, watch a movie or a television show. Remember *Maude*? The sitcom? I wanted her to be Maude and she would be content playing Maude's maid. And she apparently must have believed that men were supposed to cheat on their wives since she refused to acknowledge what was disturbingly clear: my father was a womanizer. As long as he'd show up for holidays and birthdays, smiling for pictures she'd compulsively paste into photo albums, documenting her version of a happy family, all was forgiven. I felt a lack of respect for both of them, verging on hatred, and I couldn't wait to graduate from high school, leave home, and pursue a life, a life that in no way resembled theirs. And I succeeded. Worked my way through college. Scholarships. Student loans. And zoomed to the top of my field in advertising. I wound up in New York, living in a fabulous townhouse overlooking Central Park. I had an interior decorator and a full-time housekeeper. A stylist who shopped for me. A hairdresser who came to me. A salary that wouldn't stop. I dated. Mostly white men, some of them kinda famous. All of them rich. By the time I turned forty, I was suicidal. Empty, alone, depressed. Empty, empty, empty. Alone, alone, alone. Depressed, depressed, depressed. I had to find help or I would collapse. Or explode. After a few years of intense therapy, I began the process of reprioritizing my life and finally admitted that I wanted to be a mother. More than anything. Everywhere I looked, it seemed, there were families with their newborn babies. Holding a baby was suddenly more important than any amount of success or money or prestige. I wanted to be a mommy. I wanted a family. I left New York and found a less stressful job in a quieter city. I spent more money on therapy than clothes and furniture. I began dating black men. I eventually reconciled with my parents, now well into their seventies. And, like I was living out a fairy tale, I met Ralph. A man who was so different from any man I'd ever met. Sensitive. The kind of man any woman would want to be the father of their child—smart, funny, caring, and loyal. And Ralph has this pride as a black man that is perceptible but not angry. I knew he was the family man I desired. We got married. I'm pregnant! After what seemed like an eternity, I got pregnant. Neither of us is particularly sexual so it took some energy. But it finally happened. I thought my age might be the problem but we pulled it off. In fact, at this very moment Ralph is out picking up baby furniture. I stayed home to paint the baby's room. Ralph can't believe I'm insisting on painting it myself. With this belly in the way. Sometimes I feel the baby kick, a shock that reminds me I'm pregnant. It's amazing to think about how far I've come. I'm not saying I'm totally well or anything. Believe me, I struggle. Like right now, he was supposed to be back from the furniture store about a half an hour ago. I begin to worry. And it inevitably brings up thoughts of my father. Who was always late. Fear. You know. But then I feel the baby move inside me, and remember that Ralph is not my father. Ralph is a good man. He's just late. That husband of mine refuses to wear a watch. No sense of time. The baby is due in three months. I've told him to call when he's going to be late but he doesn't. The room is yellow. A bright, sunny yellow. Yellow is my mother's favorite color. Yellow is so hopeful, so optimistic.

BARRIERS

Louise

Louise is a mental health professional in her fifties.

I was in the midst of doing a class when Billy came in and said, "Angel is out on the porch and he's hyperventilating." Some people called him Joey; some people called him Angel. He was kneeling, crouched over, and breathing so fast that it was unbelievable. I leaned down and said, "Angel, are you having a severe panic attack?" I've had severe panic attacks so I just assumed that's what he was having. I tried to get him to slow his breathing. He was just freaked out. Scared to death, like a little animal. And I felt so sorry for him because I know what it's like. It's horrible, absolutely horrible. You feel like a lion is chasing you but there's no lion. Nothing was working. He did not want to move or lie down; he was so distressed. Sweating like a pig. Billy pulled me aside and said, "Three days ago, Angel had a really bad panic attack and afterwards he stuck scissors into his arm and cut himself." We called 911 and they came and helped him calm down. I gave him some tranquilizers. We tried to get him to go to the hospital but he had no desire to go. If we pushed him to go, it seemed for certain that he would have another panic attack. So after the 911 brigade left, I brought him some water since he was dehydrated and sat with him for about a half an hour. Then I did this thing called "contracting," making a verbal contract with him. I said, "Angel, you agree to come to me if you feel like you want to kill yourself. This is our contract, okay? Find me or someone on the staff. Promise?" About five minutes later, Billy came running in and said, "Angel's tongue is blue." As soon as I heard him say those words, I said, "Call 911." I ran down the hall to the area where the men have their cubicles. Joey was lying there, partially covered by some shirts. There was a pole above him, only about four—three and a half?—feet from the floor, where he hung his clothes. I had to dig in there—that's just what you do—to assess the situation. There was crap everywhere, like he was practically buried. Among other things, there were several black-and-white glossy photographs of Carmen Miranda from some of her movies. It seems you never really know anyone until after they die. There was a leather belt around his neck, intricately and skillfully looped around the pole. Only later did I realize that I had made a mental note that something seemed out of place about the belt. It didn't match the shirts that were strewn about or the shoes he was wearing. I don't mean match like in color coordination. It just stood out; the belt seemed to be breathing even though Joey wasn't. Does that sound crazy? I'm from the old school. A nurse does every-thing to save a life. Vomit is nothing. Nothing. Sure, it was everywhere—copious amounts of vomit. On my clothes. In my hair. My nose. My mouth. I wasn't thinking about whether or not he was HIV-positive. I do remember thinking that he was in his twenties, same as my two boys, my sons. He looked like my oldest son. I had one of those barriers in my purse—a piece of plastic with a hole in it that you're sup-posed to put over their mouth during CPR. I bought one—a barrier—for six bucks. Comes in a cute little pouch that was somewhere in my purse. At that point, did I even know where my purse was? When most people hang themselves, they do it from a certain height so their feet can't touch the floor. Joey was just slumped over. He had to force himself, force himself to stop breathing. That's why people step off a chair—so there's no turning back. Even if the mind says you want to die, the body takes over. It's hard to fight the body's desire to survive. In most hanging cases, when the person jumps, they break their neck—that's what kills them. Joey's neck wasn't broken. He strangled himself with all his might. He really wanted to die. He had an ongoing romance with death, finally consummated. I cried most of the day on Saturday, fearing that I'd go back into my own black hole. While I have no idea how it feels to be homeless or locked up in prison or abandoned by my family, I understood his pain. You have no idea how much respect and admiration I have for them. Listen, I had a certain privilege at birth—call it luck, whatever—or I would be dead. They were not born lucky. I spoke to his father on the phone. He was sobbing uncontrollably. There were so many barriers between them— Joey's sexuality, his drug use, his mental illness. His father asked if he could come and get Joey's things. A television, a DVD player, clothes, a few books, those Carmen Miranda pictures. He asked if there was any money. There was, and we gave it to him. We had gotten rid of the gay porn magazines. And I don't quite know how to explain something I did. Intuitively. This is difficult to admit and I don't really have an explanation. I took the belt. His belt. I stuffed it in my purse when no one was looking. Something made me. Something told me to take it. Only later that evening did I realize there was dried vomit on it. I cleaned it, the belt covered with Joey's dry puke and my wet tears. I found a box, a pretty box, and put the clean belt in it. I placed the box in a special drawer where I keep all my treasures—photos of my family, cherished letters, trinkets from cities I've visited. The drawer is a storehouse of memories that keep me alive. That's where Joey's belt belongs.

Gina

Gina, fortyish, is a black former street hooker and drug addict on the mend.

First thing I remember bein' called was "Piggy." Then "nigger." Then "slightly retarded." A slightly retarded nigger piggy: that's what I was, I guess. Only recently did I find out I am schizoaffective. A schizoaffective slightly retarded nigger piggy recovering drug addict. And I don't care who knows it. I was born premature. I wasn't supposed to live past six. My mama gave me to my grandma so she could run off and chase her dreams. My mama said she didn't believe my daddy was my daddy. My brother and me lived with my grandma on this land—right up against this home where they put mens when they got released from prison and the nuthouse. Those mens called me "Piggy" 'cause I was fat and always tryin' to get somethin' from 'em. They taught me some things, these mens—how to lie, steal, forge checks. I was good at all that but I flunked first grade. All you gotta do is eat and sleep and play but I flunked. I was one of the first black kids to go to a integrated school. About the sixth grade. They called me "nigger" but then they'd play with me. There was a white teacher who was real good to me but they fired him because he wasn't supposed to be givin' any attention to blacks. After taking one of them tests they gives, that's when they decided I was "mildly retarded" and needed some medication. I tried to go to a school where they prepare you for work but they kicked me out when they found out I was mildly retarded. My people couldn't afford no medicines. My grandma cleaned houses. When she wasn't whippin' me. That's all you could do if you was black—clean houses, fast food, mow lawns. My brother went to school, and when he finished, he and his buddy went in the service together, then they got kicked out of the service together, and moved to Miami together. He was my only family. Mine. My other brothers and sisters had different daddies but Carl was my flesh and blood. My mama's flesh. We looked like twins. You look at Carl, you see me. You look at me, you see Carl. He was mine. My brother, he wanted me to come to Miami. I planned it every day, thought about it constantly. My dream was to be in Miami with my brother, my flesh. Mine. I wound up goin' to Miami. But not to see my brother. We got a call, saying he got shot. His friend—the one he went to school with, went to service with, went to Miami with—shot him. To death. He was on drugs but my brother wasn't. My brother was into the Bible. So I went to Miami to hunt him down. I found him and just stared him down. When you looks at me, you looks at my brother. "I'm sorry," he said, over and over. That's all I did: stared at him with my brother's face. After a few days, I went to find him, just to remind him what he done, and there he was in an alley with a needle hangin' outa his arm. Dead. That was justice. Right after that was when I got married. I was thirteen. My husband, like those mens at my grandma's, taught me some things. Like whorin' and doin' porno. Robberies. I danced in clubs. I was still in that naïve stage where I believed I was to "love and cherish" my husband "until death does us apart"—even though he was a pimp. I got pregnant. Had miscarriages 'cause he beat me; sometimes he shook me so hard that he killed the baby inside me. I had my first little girl when I was fourteen. More miscarriages. More babies. Theys slow, my kids. I finally left him for a Cuban drug dealer who made me watch him have sex with his bitches. One night he beat me real bad. I had to go to the hospital with my cracked body. After I got out, I gots him real drunk and stole his money. Then I takes my kids and went to Baton Rouge. That's when I started snortin' crack, baby, and workin' the streets. I'd work at KFC in the day, take off that uniform, and put on my nighttime outfit: real short skirt, split up the front, no panties, no brassiere, big high heels. Put on my Walkman and move to the music. When I get into that music, I don't see nobody—until a car pulls up. I needed to make about $100 a day. Five tricks. Honey, I know every nationality and what they likes. Black mens like head. Mexicans like fucking—especially when they drunk. Those Chinese like to stick their fist in your coochie—see if it fits. I seen it all. Some of them motherfuckers would try to talk me down to $5. So I'd just kinda stick my body in the car without actually gettin' in. "You want head for $5, baby?" Then they'd hand me a five dollar bill, and I'd kiss 'em on the top of the head, and I'd split. My back is all scarred from the times I scrapped it, making my escapes. I give you head, all right. For five fuckin' dollars. I done lotsa jail time—90 days, 150 days, a total of about eight years. In prison, you'd see these womens who looks like theys pure men—they walks like men, they talks like men. Like Billy Dee Williams. Or Eddie Murphy. But no dick. In jail, you cry, you gets horny, you have wet dreams, and you have fights. I tried sleepin' my way through jail time. One day I gets a call from my mother, tellin' me that my daddy wants to see me. Out in Los Angeles. The daddy who didn't think I was his. I gets there and what do I get? A lecture, tellin' me I will abide by his rules. But no hug. Daddy got me a factory job and charged me rent. It was boring. So back to the streets where it was fun. I likes my truck drivers. One put on my panties. One of 'em like to wear my stockins while I runs around the truck nude. That was right up my alley—I like them freaks. Moved out from my Daddy and learned to smoke crack cocaine. That's when things took off. I got hooked bad on the rock. Lowered myself. I did crack right next to the garbage can, behind the garbage can. Inside the garbage can. I pimp my friends for crack. Then that pipe start pimpin' me. That pipe makes you bow down to its level. When I come here to get better, these peoples saw somethin' in me I didn't know I had. Now I know I likes people and I love to involve myself.

So I'm leadin' some NA meetins for womens even though I still think I talk like a country girl. I'm workin' a real job with peoples whose been where I been. I'm there for them, baby, and they there for me. First time I ever wanna stay clean and sober. Take responsibility. I gotta idea for a sitcom of my life. Miss Diana Ross can play me.

Edward

Edward is a mentally ill but stabilized drug addict and street person who insists he isn't gay in spite of being a male hustler.

Mentally ill. Paranoid. Hustler. Depressed. AIDS. Straight. Suicidal. Jailbird. Hard-headed. Pothead. And schizoaffective. I was born in San Bernadino. My father left before I arrived. My mother didn't protect me like a mother should. When I was a teenager, she disappeared. Poof. Vanished. Into thin fuckin' air. My mom told me so many lies about my dad that I have no fuckin' idea who he is. Truth is I don't think she knows. The accident happened when I was about twelve or thirteen. My mom was passed out cold in the back seat. One of her boyfriends was driving, totally drunk. I was in the front passenger seat and saw it comin'. He crashed into a stop sign. It practically cut the car in half. I was hurt the worst. Both my legs broken. And some kind of concussion. It's when my problems started. Missed a buncha school and never caught up. Then started skipping school. Her boyfriend was history. Only thing I liked about him was that she'd stay outta my bed when he was around. The minute he split, she started up again. Why didn't she pick my brother? The smell of her—all sweet perfume and stale booze made me sick to my stomach. She didn't know how to be a mother, treatin' me like a boyfriend. When another boyfriend showed up, I was relieved. Kinda. I'd go from gettin' too much attention to no attention. Decided to run away. Packed my things and stole the new boyfriend's car. My first auto theft. I didn't get very far. Maybe 60 or 70 miles out of town and they pull me over. I wasn't old enough to have a driver's license. Since everyone agreed there was somethin' wrong with me, they didn't prosecute me. The judge ordered me to go to church and confess my sins at least once a week. He said because I wasn't "all well," I'd sin more than most people. The priest used me. Gave me money. I bought weed with the money he gave me. He knew no one would believe me if I told on him. He let me know I was hopeless and tried to make me turn gay. But I got away from him. And her. I had to. The streets—any streets in any city—were safer than bein' in the same small town as my mother and the priest. When I left, about 30 years ago, I vowed I'd go back to San Bernadino and kill both of them fuckers. Changed my plans a little. I'm only gonna kill him. I moved to San Diego. Lived in the park. Hustled. Slept on park benches. Smoked dope. Had sex in cars, the park, wherever. It was okay. Even though I was high and hungry, paranoid and depressed. Sometimes suicidal. When I got older and wiser, I started movin' on up. Spent several years in New Orleans. Worked out of a bar in the French Quarter. Got me a hotel room. Made enough money to buy me some clothes. I'd make three or four hundred dollars a day. Six tricks or so. They'd give me head or I'd fuck 'em. Sometimes a thou, depending. You gotta play it by ear. If they were payin' by the hour, I'd just stall 'em. Some of them chicken hawks couldn't even get it up. I'd fantasize about women. I'm straight. I'm not gay. I never was gay. I'm bein' honest. Doin' all that sex shit made me feel scummy and demoralized. Screwed me up. Thinkin' people are all out to get me. When I was in jail, I was considered fresh meat. Insteada money, I had sex for cigarettes, sex for candy bars. But never sex for fun. Never gay sex. About seven years total in prison. The next big event was 1994. Got that AIDS test. I was in some psych ward, which was nothing unusual, and they asked me if I'd been tested for AIDS 'cause I had the flu bad. First thing I thought about was my promise to eradicate the world of that cocksucking priest. Wonder if I'd have enough time. After that AIDS news, I started doin' crack. Up until that time, I'd only done marijuana. But the crack thing just happened and

I was into it. Moved to L.A. Shame. Constant shame. Since the priest turned me into damaged goods. I remember he shot his load on my hand one time. Cum all over my fuckin' hands. There was no turning back after that. It poisoned me for good. Made me wanna throw up. Disgusted me. I'm not gay. Out there they fill you fulla shit. Tell you that you're hot and you're believin' it. Doesn't everybody? I ate it up. I was in the game. Never loved someone. I need to learn how to love someone. Trying not to manipulate people any more. I haven't run outta hope. I'm tryin' to stop. Cut way back. Quit crack. Quit cigarettes, too. But still into my weed. I've had a terrible life but I'm less depressed now, that's for sure. Since I been here. It takes a lot of work to change your life.

Ricky

Ricky is a Hispanic, gay professional in the field of recovery and mental illness; flamboyant but not without depth.

The first thing I did, after I got the call, was searched my apartment for that photo of my little drag diva, as Carmen. It was the only photo I ever saw of Joey where he really seemed happy. Even in photographs, you could tell he was uncomfortable, like he wanted to jump out of his skin. I could not fucking find that goddamn photograph. I probably should have been crying or something more appropriate under the circumstances, but nooooo, I'm looking everyfuckingwhere for an old photograph—in my underwear drawer, this box where I keep special things, that locked filing cabinet that my will is in. Did I give that photo back to him? I wanted to see him alive. Happy. I'd actually seen him that morning. That Friday morning. His last day on the planet. I was raised by nuns, honey. And not a Julie Andrews type among 'em. But what I learned, attending a traditional Catholic school, was to be selfless. I'm not particularly religious but being of service is just an extension of what Sister Mary This and Sister Mary That drummed into our impressionable little brains. I never considered myself an activist but I've always been concerned with social justice. I was in the HIV/AIDS field for fourteen years before coming here to Skid Row. Most people have put up barriers that separate them from Skid Row. Barriers that separate them from us. No one is "from" Skid Row, so the question is, How did they get here? The one thing about Skid Row is that it makes you look at yourself. It's like a big funhouse mirror in front of your face without the proper lighting. In my work, and in my life, I like to practice what I call The Art of Engagement. When I meet someone, I want it to matter. Joey was a child when he came here. Beautiful. But I wasn't sure he could make a fist, let alone survive. We had an immediate rapport; he was just so open. We play different roles here and I'm an openly gay man so, after finding out that Joey lost his mother at a very early age, I assumed the role of his Mom. Mamacita Ricky. Then there were the procession of boyfriends. I'd insist that he bring them in for Mamacita's inspection. Some of them were okay with that but a couple of 'em said it was "sick." "That's okay, honey," I'd say, "just have a seat." Most of them were not good enough for my Joey. But he never saw himself the way I saw him, the way others saw him. He has this abundance of energy. To see him dance was an experience. He'd get a boom box and create a stage with some orange crates and proceed to put on a show. When he danced, it was almost as if he was trying to jump out of his skin, escape from the body he so despised—like he was on fire or something. You could not get that kid to sit still. He was a computer whiz and he'd come in and help me copy and collate like a dervish. I called him my little Girl Friday. He was an open book. Most people here take years to open up but he just let his entire story spill out: Alcohol and marijuana use began when he was fifteen, followed by acid, cocaine, crystal meth, and heroin. Diagnosed as bipolar, ADHD, and paranoid schizophrenic. Occasional cross-dresser. Hustler. Anorexic. Bulimic. Gay. Bisexual. Talk about your shock and awe. Shall I continue? Raped at gunpoint, a history of self-mutilation, tried to kill himself several times. A father who routinely beat the shit out of him. To tell you the truth, I've pretty much blocked that day out. I had gone home and received a message from Louise, saying it was "urgent." I called back and whoever answered the phone told me. Only three words: "Joey is gone." We always wanted to protect him, take care of him. He came into our lives for a reason. What is it that we learn from each other? Somebody, please tell me. I felt this profound sadness but I didn't even cry. When I woke up on Saturday morning, I was totally numb. No tears. Did Carmen Miranda commit suicide? Or was it booze? Something. I feel like a father who has lost his son.

MAKE LOVE NOT WAR

Lou

Lou is a widower in his sixties who lost his son in the 9/11 tragedy.

I'd just about given up, heart broken, unable to mend. Days become weeks become months become years. I resented the hoopla at every anniversary. I resented the media and the masses grabbin' a hold of my pain. Get your own tragedy. This one is mine, all mine, and no you don't know what it feels like. The call came three years, two months, and five days after. After September One-one, 2001. The girl's voice said, "Mr. Jacobs? We've identified your son." These were the words I had waited for; the words that would let me go to sleep, the words that would slow down my heartbeat, the words that would allow me to move on. Four words. "We've identified your son." I visited Andy down there, at Ground Zero, every day for the first year. 365 days. Then I started goin' once a week on Sunday mornings. Continued. Lookin' for a sign. I just wanted to know. Know he was dead. It's important. I don't know why but it is. Sometimes, I'd sit there and see if I could hear his voice. I'd just listen. Never in my life did I believe in any of that bullshit about past lives or reincardination or any of that crap. But when you need to know about your flesh and blood, when you need to know where he is, you listen. Sometimes I'd fall asleep and wake up to the sound of a drumbeat. Or? I dunno. Maybe it was my heart pounding in my chest. Maybe a bad dream. Or just some anxiety. I refused to take any medication for my nerves. "We identified his DNA," she said, soundin' almost perky-like. "You have him there? My boy? Can I see? Can I see my boy? My Andy? Pieces of my boy? Do I make an appointment? What?" "Mr. Jacobs," she said, all traces of that business tone in her voice gone. "The DNA was found in your son's heart." I tried to take it in. Heart? Did she say his heart? Was she looking at my boy's heart? Could she touch it? The heart that cared for his sick dog one long hot summer when he was six or seven years old? The heart that fell in love with that gorgeous cheerleader when he was in high school? The heart that broke when his mother died of cancer in '99? "Did you say that the DNA was found in his heart? That's how you know? That's how you know it's him? My boy? My Andy?" "Yes, Mr. Jacobs," she said, and then added somethin' that I betcha isn't part of the formal procedure. "It's the first time I've ever heard of it," she said, barely above a whisper. "First time I ever heard of a heart providing proof of identification." And then she said, "It's kind of beautiful. At least I think so." My boy's heart endured; my boy's heart caught up with me. Someone once said to me, "Your son Andy is all heart." I think it was a teacher in elementary school. "All heart"—that's what she said. My son Andy: all heart.

Ted Junior

Ted Junior is an American Vietnamese veteran of the Iraqi war, living on Skid Row.

My dad was convinced that the war would make a man out of me. The last resort. Make a man out of me. You'd be surprised how many things he thought would make a man out of me. It was his mission to make his son a man, constructed in his image. All man. My Dad was a Vietnam vet. Marine. One tough guy. Masculine and then some. That's what everyone believed. Only I knew. Only I knew the truth. This making-a-man-out-of-me routine started when I was seven or eight years old. He'd climb into bed with me and force me to suck on his dick and swallow his cum. His manhood. "Drink it, boy," he'd say. Sometimes I'd throw up. Gag. Tears running down my face. "You need it." I needed his macho semen, he said. To make me a man. There was nothing effeminate or gay about me but he lived in fear that I'd be perceived as gay and his cover would be blown. So to speak. At some point, I stopped feeling anything. Couldn't even hate him. I played football, dated: all to please him. And always keeping his extracurricular cocksucking activities a secret. The dutiful son. Sometimes, during the nighttime visits, it was like I removed myself and watched the scene play out. As an observer, not a participant. "If you tell anyone," he'd remind me. "I'll blow your brains out." He met my mother in Vietnam. A whore. He got her pregnant as a result of a dare. I am the result. Maybe the only time they had sex. 1974. I am a bit like my mom. Small boned. A bit frail. Slightly passive, I guess. But not homosexual. Not heterosexual. Not anysexual. My mother is totally subservient to him. The relationship remains what it was when they initially met. He delivers orders. She follows—head bowed, always trying to shrink herself so that she's smaller, and when she speaks (which is rare) it is never above a jumbled whisper. He's her puppeteer; she only moves, talks, responds, eats, sleeps, when he pulls her strings. She wears what he tells her. Since the war, he has insisted that she wear all this red, white, and blue crap. Propaganda T-shirts. Then she started wearing Bush T-shirts. It's tragic. She doesn't know George Bush from George of the Jungle. And no matter how many colors of the flag decorate her broken body, she is not in any way an American. As a kid, I had a hard time saying the Pledge of Allegiance or singing the national anthem. Just because I've seen *E.R.* and I know who Donald Trump is, I do not feel American. This is not my country. Not my sweet land of liberty. My father wouldn't allow me to study the things that interested me—architecture or literature. "Sissy courses," he'd hiss at me. I wound up not going to college. No escape. Of course he didn't want me to go away to school. He didn't want to lose his sex toy. My mother and I were held hostage and expected to take care of his piggish needs. When George Bush declared war, there was finally something my father and I agreed on. Because my father feared that I'm going to wind up like my mother; or maybe because my father feared that I'm going to wind up like him; war was the answer. He believed going to war would make a man out of me and I saw going to war as a way to escape. He expected me to come back a man; I expected *not* to come back. While there, during boot camp, the dreams and nightmares began. It was as if my father was there with me in those barracks, still waking me in the night, forcing me to have sex. At gunpoint. Porno sex. But now I fight back. Almost killed some guy; almost strangled him to death; this guy who swore he never laid a hand on me. On the battlefield, everything was oddly familiar. Stories I'd heard him tell, Vietnam War stories, played out exactly like I'd heard them described. There were times I actually thought I was in Vietnam, not in Iraq, and I was trying to kill my own, kill my self, kill my

Vietnamese self. You don't actually know what it feels like to bang a hammer onto your head unless you do it. You don't know what the war in Iraq is like unless you are part of it—in it, smelling it, tasting it, hearing it. Sometimes I'd watch myself, same as with my dad, like I was starring in a war movie. More incidents. Freak outs. Anxiety attacks. Nervous breakdowns. Visits to the psychiatrist. One too many of these incidents and I was discharged. Honorably. The army did not make a man out of me; I returned to the foreign soil of America, not manlier, just nuttier. They sent me to a place they called home, unannounced, earlier than anticipated, catching my father off guard. I'd been replaced by some white masculine kid who was hired, according to my father, to take care of my mother while I was fighting for our country. I knew better and he knew I knew. There was nothing to do but run away, as far from Minnesota as I could. I'd be safer on the streets. Homeless? I'd always been homeless—every second of my life. Never safe, not for one minute. I convinced my mother to give me some money and took a bus to L.A. I had nightmares, bad, real bad, on the bus trip across country. War movies mixed with porno movies that I could not shut off. When I got to L.A., I tried to get some help at the V. A. Hospital. They diagnosed me with PTSD. Twice, in fact. The sex and the war. Double post-traumatic stress disorder. I tried to learn about it at the library where I'd spend much of my time, reading, and trying to educate myself so I could get a job. Get a life. I read about my illness, read that PTSD has been around for more than a hundred years. In 1871, an Army medic wrote about veterans returning home with Irritable Heart, also known as shell shock or combat neurosis. Then they changed the name to Soldier's Heart. Does that mean I still have a heart? Livin' on Skid Row. A lot like livin' in Iraq. Survival of the fittest. Tryin' to take my medication. Tryin' to find out who I am. Tryin' to stop the memories that play over and over like an X-rated movie in my head. Without end. I'd kill myself except I don't know who my self is.

Mrs. Gonzales

Lucille Gonzales is a Latin woman in her late fifties who has lost her son in the war in Iraq.

There is nothing more frustrating to me than the sound of a phone ringing and ringing off the hook ringing. No answer. My imagination starts hopping around, like a jackie rabbit, trying to come up with an explanation. No answer. Ringing, ringing, ringing. He doesn't have an answering device, my ex-husband, so I can't even leave a message. He always, always, answers before the third ring. He knows that I call with e-mail messages from our son, the soldier. Ricardo Jr. In fact, I was sitting by the computer with his most recent email on the screen. I hung up, dialed again. No answer. Maybe something is wrong with the phone. Ricardo (that's he name, also the name of my son) doesn't have a computer. I, on the other hand, am thinking of getting one of those blueberries. My ex-hubby? No computer, no answering machine, no email. Not too good in the communications department. Which is why we got divorced. After thirty years of marriage, we just totally stopped. Totally. We stopped talking to each other. I don't even remember the exact reason. Something between us died. Dead as a doorknob. To tell you the truth, we talk more now than we did when we were husband and wife. Especially since we are both missing our son. As long as the phone keeps ringing, I keep writing stories in my head. I see him, my ex-husband, suffering. In pain, great pain. And unable to get to a phone. I can't help myself. I imagine him—the only man I ever loved—dead. A heart attack perhaps. Or a stroke. Even though he stopped smoking, I cannot imagine what that man eats since we got divorced. If he lived closer, I'd hop in the car. But sixty miles is no short trip. I must have dialed his number, over and over, for twenty-five minutes or so because suddenly I realized that—except for the glow of my computer screen, it was pitch black in *mi casa*. I was frightened, even more frightened, alone in the dark. I began turning on every light in the place so that I felt safer. As I was about to switch on the front porch light, the phone rang. "Ricardo? Where have you been?" I cannot possibly describe what I heard next. News delivered from the voice of a total stranger. I thought to myself, could it be a prank? Some sick person's idea of a joke? Imagine if you can. Imagine. Imagine hearing that your husband, your ex-husband, is in jail and that your son is dead. Husband, jail. Son, dead. Same sentence. "Hi, Mom. Things are pretty good. No gory details today. Gonna lighten things up for a change." I sit and read the words on the computer screen, over and over, proving to myself that Ricky is still alive. Talking to me. I hear his voice. "I been meaning to tell you how my buddies over here laugh their asses off when I tell them my parents are named Lucille and Ricardo. Most of them think I'm trying to be funny. They can't believe it. I assure them that you are not a wacko redhead who wants to be in show business. I also tell them that you and dad stayed married way longer than the TV characters. And I let them know—in case they ever meet you—that you prefer to be called 'Lucille,' and not 'Lucy.' Thought you'd like that. Gonna sign off now. Don't worry about me, Mamacita. I'm doin' what I'm supposed to be doin': servin' my country. Tell the old man that I said hello. Love you, Lucy. LOL. Seriously, Mamacita, I love you. Your Soldier Boy, Rick." A lot has happened between the day of that stranger's call and this very moment. Ricardo and I buried our son. In a cemetery where we'd purchased three plots when we were newlyweds. Why three? We were so young and so naïve that we could have been talked into almost anything. *Tres.* It's odd. Maybe the person who sold us those gravesites was clarabuoyant. How could we have possibly imagined that one day we would be standing at those three graves, saying goodbye to our boy, as they shoveled dirt into his grave? An official musician from the army was there, playing the bugle—that song, what's it called? Tips? Taps? Tops?—the song that makes you cry even harder. After the burial, Ricardo and I needed to be alone. Friends and relatives went their separate ways and we went to dinner at a restaurant that used to be one of our favorites. We must have talked for hours. About everything, remembering details from the day we met to the present. I guess we didn't want to wait until we were dead to lie down with each other. I don't remember whose idea it was. Or if there was a choice. It just happened. Naturally. We made love. For the first time in more than ten years, we made love. At first I felt like we were disrespecting the memory of our boy. But suddenly, as I kissed every inch of Ricardo's body, feeling him inside me, I realized that we were honoring our son. Celebrating his life. I have never been so happy. Or so sad. Ricardo and I haven't spent a night apart since and that was over two years ago. We're going to get married, re-married, soon. I just need to lose a few more pounds so I can get into my wedding dress. The one I wore when we first buttoned the knot. In 1960. Before John Kennedy was assassinated. Before the war in Vietnam. Before *Dynasty* and *Dallas*. 1960. Before answering machines and George Bush Sr. and email and George Bush Jr. Thirteen or fourteen more pounds and it's back down the aisle. And this time, I promise it will be "until death do us part." *Hasta la muerte nos separe.*

Joe

Joe is a 52-year-old macho man with a secret, who served his country in Vietnam and Iraq.

I am proud to be an American. I'm proud to be a redneck, livin' in a house behind a white picket fence in a blue-collar neighborhood in a red state. I'm proud to be a Christian. I am proud to be a conservative. I'm proud to be a Republican. I'm proud to be a red-blooded white, blue-ribbon heterosexual male. I am proud to have killed for my country. I am proud to have been a marine in the Vietnam War. And I am proudest to have enlisted in the National Guard at 52 fuckin' years old, to fight in Iraq. I got what they call "killer instinct." My twin brother had it too. Ever since we was kids. Joey and Jimmy. Our dad's name was John but everyone called him Johnny. Joey (that's me) and Jimmy (my twin) and Johnny (my dad). And believe you me, the first letter of our names wasn't the only thing that we shared. Killer instinct is what made me a war hero. And it's why my brother Jimmy refuses to die. Jimmy and I did everything together so immediately upon graduatin' from high school, inspired by our Daddy who served in World War II, we enlisted to go to Vietnam. But Jimmy nearly didn't make it. One of those Viet Cong mortar attacks that took down a lot of American boys. My twin brother survived, because he's a fighter and he's got our daddy's genes, but he's pretty much a goner. Still alive, yeah, but can't walk, can't talk, can't think, can't do a fuckin' thing for himself. Doesn't recognize me; when you don't recognize your identical twin brother, your mirror image, you know there's a problem. Nam robbed me of my twin brother and gave me this, this . . . I don't have the word to describe him. "Monster," maybe? There's a picture of us taken in Nam, taken a few days before the attack that fucked him over. It's like someone ripped that picture apart and ripped my heart apart along with it. The twin brothers no longer existed. The mirror was shattered. When we realized it was unlikely Jimmy would ever be normal, like-me normal, my daddy sat me down and told me that I had to be two men, not one. Two sons. In order to carry on our family tradition and maintain our family's values, I had to take on the strength and power and the glory that my twin brother Jimmy left on that battleground. Our family name cannot be tarnished. I cannot allow my father's heart to be broken a second time. A vendetta is what it is. Hasn't our family endured enough? I won't be discredited by a bunch of lezzie lefties in leisure suits who need to get laid. Some fringe element will not succeed in harrassin' me. Over some fantasy trip. These bulldykes who wanna tear me down are the same tanks who show up at the Right to Life rallies. No real woman believes in murderin' an innocent baby. Obliteratin' a human life for selfish reasons. Abortion rights? The right to kill? Ever heard of self-control? It's all about self fuckin' control. Women don't have self control. Fags don't have self control. And several minorities don't have a shred of self-control. You know who they are. You know who you are. Now who does have self-control? George W. Bush—twice elected President of these United States—he has self-control. He stopped boozin' for Chrissake. That's proof right there. And me? I am the fuckin' epitome of self-control. That's why these fuckin' accusations are laughable. You know what the opposite of self-control is? Billyboy Clinton. No self-control whatsoever. Out of control. And that so-called wife? The future President? This is precisely what's wrong with America—to suggest in the wildest stretch of anyone's imagination that a woman could be president. A woman president? Anti-Christian. Anti-establishment. Anti-American. This is what is destroying America—a country where women want to be men and castrated pussy-boys are lettin' 'em. Going to seminars where they pound on drums and cry like little wounded girls. Fuck that Doctor Phil, motherfucker. And Deprick Chopra. And that asswipe Oprah. Propafuckin'ganda. The lawyer who is representing the little broad next door is a female attorney. She might as well have the words "female attorney" embroidered across her flat chest. Missy female attorney hates men—especially real men like me who got testosterone pourin' outta their assholes. This female attorney took the case because she believes that all men should be in jail; she believes that all men are sex freaks. Well, I'm a real man, a war hero. Two men in one, like my daddy demanded. That's me: two men for the price of one. And we all know what that must do to her: makes her wet if the truth be known. Makes her ooze. Twice. Emasculate me by playin' the molester card? Text book. The feminist agenda at play. Well, let me tell you my side of the story. Our neighbors had some domestic difficulties and the so-called man of the house moved out. His daughter—fourteen or fifteen years old, I dunno—seemed lost without daddy. So I offered to coach her so she could get on the basketball team. Out of the goodness of my heart. Her mother agreed that she needed the presence of a strong man in her life and who do you think fits that bill? So as you can imagine, it came as a big fuckin' shock when I learned that the conniving little bitch told her mommy some outlandish fantasy she obviously had and they made a police report. A police report based on wishful thinking that a war hero touched her fuckin' leg. I'm a happily married man with kids. From a substantial family. Practice self-control. I didn't touch her skinny fuckin' leg. And you know what? That will be fuckin' proven in a court of law. She rubbed her leg up against mine. This is a no brainer. Everyone is on my side—my neighbors, my congregation, my family. Who they gonna believe—this deceptive little slut who misses her daddy or me, a war hero? Twice. The charges against me will be dropped. Period. The judge is a man. We're not dealing with some loudmouth TV twat like

Judge Judy. A man will understand what men do. Or don't do. The public voted for George Bush—not once, but twice—proving that they respect men who are men. This is a country where the truth wins out. Heroes over wimps. Men over women. Good over evil. One twin over the other.

Donny

Donny is a black kid in his early twenties who was dishonorably discharged for being gay.

I didn't come out—as a gay man—on a Fire Island dance floor surrounded by members of my tribe. I came out as a gay man in Iraq. On a battlefield. No flashing disco lights and mirror balls; instead; constant deafening explosions and uncontrollable fires. Kenny was more beautiful than any girl I had dated in high school. We fell in love. A foxhole romance. Nothing about that war made sense 'cept for Kenny. Our meeting was . . . fate. He was twenty-seven years old, a few years older than me. And considerably more experienced. But he swore that he'd never been in love like this. Kenny was the first man I ever kissed. I'd messed around with guys but never kissed. First kiss. Only when I experienced his mouth exploring my mouth, his tongue licking my tongue, his beard scratching my beard. Only then did I admit I was gay. After that first kiss, there was no turning back. Our kisses—hidden, stolen, forbidden—were proof of our queer, don't-ask-don't-tell love. The two of us, together as one, represented the opposite of war: peace, calm, resolve, and no conflict. We made war but we also made love. The most monumental fight we experienced in Iraq was the fight to love—black and white, man and man—that's the only freedom worth fighting for. Only when I admitted that I loved a man did I become a man. Killing does not make you a man. Loving is what makes you a man. You'd be amazed at our ingenuity when it came to making love, finding ourselves stealing a moment of passion in spite of—or maybe because of?—the stench of death that surrounded us. Feeling him inside me, all male, all heart, filling me with life, eclipsing the ever present smell of decaying flesh and rotting bodily fluids. Kenny smelled sweet—his sweat, the inside of his mouth, his beautiful dick—all of him, every inch smelled like candy. Like a seductive sugary valentine. My war buddy, my first lover, smelled alive and he gave me that life. Man to man. Black and white. Brothers, united. First kiss. Last kiss. The day it happened we were patrolling a section of Baghdad in three Humvees. I don't know how we got separated (we usually managed to stay together in situations like this) but I was in the first Humvee and Kenny was in the third. There was an explosion and the lieutenant was yelling for us to get back to the base because we were coming under fire. I looked back and the third Humvee, the one Kenny was in, was gone. Disappeared. So I jumped out and began running down the street, running like a madman in search of the missing Humvee, in search of my missing soldier. Running, running, running, until I found what remained. The remains. The force of the explosion had practically blown the Humvee into bits, along with everyone in it. Along with Kenny. What was left of his body—and, believe me, parts were missing, totally missing—was soaked in blood, still warm. But no breath. No breath whatsoever. His lips were moist. I had to kiss him. Had to. Had to kiss him goodbye. Nothing, no one could stop me. Kissing him was not a choice. Every kiss was mandatory. Every kiss was urgent. Every kiss was required. "What the fuck are you doin'?" one of my fellow soldiers shouted as I lifted Kenny into my arms. "What the fuck are you doin', nigger?" His blood was seeping out of his body onto mine. I wanted my brother's blood inside me. As my lips touched his, as I began to kiss Kenny, I felt the first kick. "What the fuck are you doin', nigger-faggot?" I did not stop. Could not stop. Neither could he. Now each accusation he barked was accompanied by a kick. "What the fuck (kick-kiss) are you doin' (kick-kiss), sicko nigger (kick-kiss), faggot psycho (kick-kiss)?" I would die with him, the sweet taste of his blood inside me.

The next thing I remember hearing were the words "dishon-orable discharge," followed by the label of disgrace. "You are a disgrace to your country, a disgrace to manhood, a disgrace to your race, a disgrace to the human race." Branded with disgrace. I returned to Atlanta, my hometown, not with a Purple Heart but with a purple reputation. Black and purple do not go together like black and blue. Being a queer nigger is something to be hidden at all costs and I failed badly at that. My secret was out and I had nothing to lose. My honor had officially been taken from me. Even though Kenny was my only male sexual experience, I knew I was gay. I got a job in a gay bookstore (one of the few places that would have me) walking distance from my parents' house where I'm living until I get on my feet. My mother and father have been amazingly supportive. On the way to work one day, I noticed some of my kind—gay kind, that is—nervously encircling around the men's room in a little park. Before I went to Iraq, I had walked by that park hundreds, maybe thousands, of times but this was the first time I ever saw the brigade of men. Surely this wasn't the first day they decided to congre-gate there. Ever since that first experience—I went in the john and got a blowjob from a blond white boy—I haven't missed a day. Rain or shine, I visit that rancid-smelling men's room, reeking of bodily fluids, to have gay sex, over and over again, sex in every flavor and in every position. I began leav-ing for work about fifteen minutes early so I knew there would be time to get off. Then I started going to my place of worship—to worship and be worshipped—during my lunch hour. After work too. Sometimes I'd have three orgasms in one day and every single time, the same thing took place in my head. No matter what was being done to me—getting sucked, getting fucked, you name it—I would close my eyes and remember Kenny—how he smelled, how he tasted, how he felt. I was using those guys to summon memories of my dead lover. I didn't love any of those sex junkies. They were merely arteries to my grief. Cummin' instead of cryin'. Tears of semen, shooting in their eager mouths, on their hard nipples, up their hungry asses. Fillin' 'em with hot wet tears. They obviously had lots to cry about too. Because they shed their cum tears all over me, inside and out, tears running down my throat, tears spurting up my butt, tears drenching my chest. Sometimes our tears melted into each other, creating a pool of pain and fear and anger and sadness. A suicidal pool that will eventually kill us; we will drown in our collective mix of toxic juices, confirming our poisonous natures. You wanna talk about dishonorable discharges? The john is now my war zone and I will surely be among its casualties. Then and only then will I find peace, reunited with my Kenny, my lover, my soldier.

Mr. Gonzales

Mr. Gonzales is a Latin man in his early sixties who lost his only son in the Iraqi war.

I voted for the prick. Twice. We live in Texas. Not votin' for Dubya would have been some kind of a sacrilege. For a Texan. Kinda like a Mexican not gettin' drunk on Cinco de Mayo. I can forgive myself for the first time. But the second time? I don't know. Maybe I was tryin' to convince myself that there was a reason for Ricardo Jr. to go to war. He sure believed in the war. Loved bein' a soldier, like a little kid playin' make believe. He had guts, that's for sure. Told people he was willing to die for his country. They signed him up at the local mall, a few weeks after he graduated from high school. They promised him he would not be in combat; they promised him that he would be able to get a college degree. He felt like he was chosen. He was chosen, all right. Because he had dark skin and because he was naïve as shit. A good boy, he kept in touch. His mamacita, after we divorced, got a computer. (Probably so she could find a new husband in one of those chit-chat rooms.) Anyway, Ricky emails her and she calls me and reads 'em, always remindin' me how backward I am 'cause I don't have a computer. But she's okay. We're better friends now than we was when we was married. She moved away, about 60 miles from me. I don't know why they chose to come to my house first (and not hers) but they did and I didn't need anybody to tell me what it means when an official government van slowly pulls up to your house in the middle of the day and a couple of suits get out and walk slowly, like they're getting' married or somethin,' up to the door. With some official lookin' papers in hand. We've seen this happen in dozens of movies. Usually there's some sappy music in the background. No music. Just the sound of one of their voices. "Mr. Gonzales, we regret to inform you. . . ." "Come in, gentlemen," I said, cutting him off before he could finish. I didn't want to hear the words. Didn't want to hear the word "son" and the word "dead" in the same sentence. They walked in, still in slow motion, as if we were already in the funeral home and my boy, Ricardo Jr., was already laid out in his casket. They gave their speech, barely above a whisper. I picked up every third word or so. "Sniper . . . Fallujah . . . intestine . . . bleeding . . . died." I excused myself, probably thinkin' I'd do the polite thing and get these slow-moving men something to drink. *Agua*, maybe. Ice water. I walked into the kitchen and right out the back door and into the backyard. I began to cry hot tears. Mexican men don't cry. I got down on the ground, the ground where Ricky took his first baby steps, the ground where we had annual Fourth of July picnics every year of his life (even when it rained like crazy), the ground where he and I got drunk on shots of tequila the night before he went to Iraq. My cries turned into wails. The sun was setting. It was getting dark. Fast. The darker it got, the louder I seemed to howl. I really don't know how or why I got in there but I found myself in the garage. Warmth, maybe. Light? I honestly don't know and I don't remember, I do not remember. I do not remember leaving the garage and walking up the driveway while those two thirsty men sat waiting for their water. In the dark house. I had a can in my hand. I headed toward the official van parked on the street. The enemy vehicle. The neighborhood streetlights hadn't come on yet so it was pretty dark. I don't remember lookin' for matches. Never carry 'em in my pocket since I stopped smokin' two years ago. I don't remember pouring the kerosene all over their fuckin' vehicle, the vehicle that belongs to the United Fucking States government. What I mostly remember is the sound. That whoosh sound. Reminds me of the sound of a blanket being shaken, fresh out of the drying machine. Sounds like flight. Whoosh.

The sound was followed by the sight, the smell, the feel, and the taste of fire. Orange flames. Crackling. Burning smells. Heat. Light. Then sirens. Fire trucks. Police cars. The men came out of the house, moving a bit more quickly now, but keeping their distance. "I ain't goin' anywhere," I promised. And I sat down, tired now. You'd think the sound of the wailing sirens would drowned out the sound of the phone ringin' inside the house but no, I could hear it. It had to be his mama callin' to tell me about Ricardo's most recent email. All I could hear was the phone. That woman would not hang up. She musta suspected something because I'm always home, home alone, and pickin' up the phone before the third ring. I just could not pick up that phone. I could not tell her that her son, the love of her life, was dead. Son, dead: same sentence. I let it ring as the cops arrived, treatin' me like I was a crazy person—a mass murderer or somethin'. The sound of water was gushing out of those huge hoses, spraying the smoking vehicle, its guts burnt out. Agua! Suddenly I remember I did not get the messengers their water. "Mr. Gonzales?" one of the cops said. "We'll make this as painless as possible but you have committed a crime. It's understandable. I understand what you must be going through." "You do?" I said. "You understand what I'm going through? What a fuckin' coincidence this is. So your son got killed in a senseless war today? Your only boy, not even twenty years old, is dead because of some motherfucking war-crazy moron called the president? If that is the case, yeah, then you understand. You understand perfectly. But. You listening to me? BUT if that is not the case, if you did not lose your nineteen-year-old flesh and blood in the war today, then fuck you. Fuck you—do you hear me? I'll say it once more. FUCK YOU. You don't understand a fuckin' thing." Handcuffs. They put me in handcuffs. Off to jail. "My wife," I said. "My *ex*-wife. Someone has to tell her. Tell her that her son is dead. Son. Dead."

Geoffrey

Geoffrey is a happily married gay man who, along with his partner, become father figures to twin boys who lose their dad in the war.

Darryl and I have been "married" for eight—no, make that nine—years. In emotional terms, anyway. Not legally. Not, perhaps, in the eyes of God depending on *who* your God is and *what* his eyes see. We live in a modest house in the burbs. Two car garage. No white picket fence but we are part of the American landscape, as American as apple pie. We are a couple, perceived as a couple by anyone who pays attention. We mow the lawn; we don't have all-night parties; even on Halloween, we don't stand out. Our neighbors on the left, the young couple with five-year-old twin boys has always been friendly but we don't hang out. Just the usual neighborly things: occasionally sign for a Fedex delivery; one year they took in our mail when we were on vacation. They've never told us what they do in bed and they've never asked us what we do in bed. Last year Darryl and I couldn't resist buying Christmas presents for the boys. Huge stuffed bears, practically life size. No big deal but it proved to be one of those bonding moments. The five-year-olds were suddenly our new best friends. Because Darryl and I look somewhat alike (the curse of narcissistic gay men who are attracted to their mirror image) and because we live together, the twins assumed that we were twins. We explained that we were really good friends. (I actually like the idea that we're twins.) Shortly after Christmas, we noticed that Jimmy, the twins' dad, was home a lot. He'd been terminated from his job. Downsizing. While looking for work without much success, he seemed to be

94

enjoying the free time with his boys. But after several months, Jimmy started to look like he was getting frustrated. Then a bit angry. One day, out of the blue, Sharon told us he had enlisted to go to Iraq. I guess it seemed like a solution to their financial situation (she had confided that they were behind in their house payments). He would learn a skill—maybe go to college—with an eye to finding something to provide his family some security down the line. Jimmy didn't say goodbye to us so we really didn't know exactly when he left. We noticed that the boys were playing by themselves and were not quite as happy as they appeared to be when their daddy was on the scene. One day, they were playing a version of war. This was not a make-believe war; this was a real war, a war that robbed them of their favorite playmate. The neighbors on our right told us. The news. It was the only time the two of them, the Mr. and Mrs., showed up at our door, unannounced. The Mrs. was holding on to the Mr. as if she was in great danger of losing him. "We don't know if you heard," he said. "But . . . ." Now the Mrs. is sobbing, holding her husband tighter as he attempts to finish his sentence above the sound of his wife's crying. "Jimmy was killed in Iraq . . . ." The Mrs. was saying—repeating, actually, over and over—"war noise, war noise." At least that's what I heard, muffled through her sobs. It's odd that I initially heard "war noise" but eventually realized that she was saying "those poor boys, those poor boys." Isn't that odd? "War noise." What does war sound like? I just couldn't let myself think about "those poor boys." Those five-year-olds without a dad. Weeks after we'd digested Jimmy's death, having attended the funeral, Darryl and I were reliving the day we learned the news, comparing notes (as married couples often do) on our impressions of the Mr. and Mrs. "I'm certain they are not Bush fans," Darryl said of the neighbors—on the right. "Inappropriately placed, in that case," I said. "What makes you so certain?" "When she kept repeating 'those poor boys, those poor boys,'" Darryl said, "she was obviously sympathiz-

ing with the military in Iraq, feeling the futility of their battle." Well, he may not have heard "war noise" but he didn't
hear what I heard. Even though the words were the same,
there was no question in my mind that she was referring to
the twins. Those poor boys. Not the poor boys on the battlefield. Those poor boys. The phrase won't leave me. It plays
like a broken record. Those poor boys. Sharon asked us to
come to dinner one night. Just the three of us since the twins
were with their grandma. We assumed it was simply because
she was lonely. Darryl and I determinedly let go of our judgment about the gargantuan American flag she had recently
hung in their front yard. Shortly after we arrived, she got
right to the point. Would Darryl and I consider playing an
active role in the twins' lives since they lost their father? They
need a consistent male presence in their lives, she explained.
"Men to look up to. Decent," she said. "Like the two of you."
Of course we agreed. We tried to be very aware of the firsts
that the twins were experiencing. First birthday without their
dad. First day of kindergarten. First holiday season. Their
school put on a Christmas pageant (I guess that's what you'd
call it although it sounds awfully faggy, doesn't it?). The twins
insisted, in fact, that we be there for the show/performance/
whatever. Sharon deliberately didn't sit with us. We think she
wants to let the boys know we are there for them, not her.
The last song they performed was called, "Let There Be Peace
on Earth." Every one of the kids had learned the words as
well as learned how to perform the accompanying sign lan-
guage. The twins, because they are pretty short, stood in
front so we could see them perfectly. "Let there be peace on
Earth," they sang. "And let it begin with me." They point,
somewhat histrionically, to themselves. Imagine the power in
those little voices, teaching us grown-ups about peace. "Let
there be peace on Earth and let it begin with me."

Performance Rights

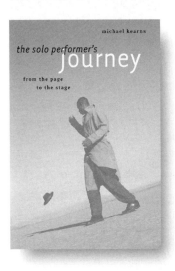